# ODD OTIS

## An Unusual Tail (Tail)

*A Special Needs Journey.....*

### By Alan & Kathi Hiatt

**Available on Amazon.com Books**

# ODD OTIS

*alanhiatt@sbcglobal.net/kathihiatt@att.net*
Photography provided by Kathi Hiatt

# Friend 'Odd Otis' on Facebook

# Dedication

We are dedicating this book to Tina, a gracious and selfless little lady who unexpectedly popped into our lives and forever changed it. Thank you from the bottom of our hearts.

*The Hiatts*

# Table of Contents

Find Odd Otis Q&A's at the back of this book

By Tina Sloan

# TINA'S TALE

*When the world says, "Give up,"*
*Hope whispers, "Try it one more time."*

Tina, a nineteen-year-old college student and volunteer at the local animal shelter lay in a motionless coma. She had been a passenger when the vehicle she was in was T-boned by an intoxicated driver.

Upon impact, Tina was thrown through the windshield and onto the pavement. Though her doctors were sure she would eventually wake from her coma, their terrible prognosis was that she would be both physically and mentally incapacitated for the rest of her life. The best they could recommend was around the clock care with confinement. But this is not where Tina's story ends, it's where it begins.

Tina was blessed with parents who refused to accept the doctor's prognosis. Her mom and dad took her home with a fierce determination and a promise to help her heal—No matter what or how long it might take. They dutifully named it *The Tina Project*.

In spite of the many years of mental and physical rehabilitation that followed, neither Tina nor her parents gave up their struggle to overcome the impossible odds. Though recovery from her brain injury had its limits, it was with unflinching determination and a strong love for each other that Tina slowly overcame the worst of her physical disabilities.

Though Tina's caring parent are always close at hand, Tina has since grown into the fiercely independent, caring, and loving woman that she is today. She still struggles with her memory and a speech problem that she says "sometimes gets all tangled up," but the accident did not deter her from her love of animals.

Unable to fulfill her long-term dream of being a veterinarian, Tina has spent her life caring for and rescuing animals. Her current rescue is Sky, her lovable Pitt Bull mix. Five years ago it was two adorable white puppies. One was blind, the other was blind and deaf.

Tina was adamant in her refusal to let the breeder put the blind and deaf puppies down. She picked them both up, put them in her car, and took them home with her; ignoring the breeders warning that the pups were never going to be anything other than an exasperating burden. "You're going to regret your decision to keep the pups," he told Tina as she drove off.

"I'm like a kid at Christmas when it comes to rescuing a dog," she says as she puts her arms around the now grown pups and gives them a squeeze.

Tina and Odd Otis' stories are strangely similar. Both were met with crippling circumstances that were beyond their control, and yet neither of them ever gave up or abandoned hope. Against all possible odds they have both strived to prove to the world how with a little bit of help, they can pretty much do anything their counterparts can do. Hence, the story of *Odd Otis* begins.

# Tina

# Odd Otis' Story

## Lost & Found

**His Version...**

I stomped on the pedal—the tires on my restored CJ7 (Jeep) screeched to halt—micro inches from the *Don't mess with Texas* sticker pasted on the bumper of the car in front of me.

"What the...?" I yelled at the moron in front of me.

Being an older model Jeep (1984) there are no airbags, but I did extend a mental thank you to General Motors for the lap belt that kept my body from slamming into the steering wheel.

SKERRRT...screamed the tires on the pickup truck behind me— fishtailing off to the side of the road.

"You idiot!" the red-faced driver of the truck shouted, shaking a balled-up fist.

Ignoring the remark about my intelligence, I peered down the road in front of me. Though I half-expected to see a traffic accident, the problem appeared to be the result of a long line of vehicles creeping slowly around some sort of obstacle lying in the middle of the road. We live in a mountain community, so road kill (skunks, raccoons, squirrels) or large hunks of firewood bouncing out of the back end of someone's truck is nothing unusual.

It wasn't until the traffic in front of me began to creep forward that I was finally able to give the rust-stained truck (the one that almost slammed into the rear end of my jeep) enough room to pull back onto the Skyway; the Skyway being the local rural highway and major roadway responsible for connecting several small mountain towns in our area.

I must have crept along at least another quarter of a mile before I finally spotted him—a long-haired, white Australian Shepherd mix crisscrossing the double yellow line in the center of the road. His being in the middle of the road was bad enough but, to make matters worse, the double yellow line he was traversing also happened to be one of the Skyway's busiest intersections.

The vehicles ahead of me were zigzagging and honking. A few of the drivers were hollering curse words out their side window, but no one was able or willing to stop for fear of endangering themselves or other drivers. Which means the 'white dog in the middle of the road' chaos made it impossible for me to pull over as well; unless, of course, I wanted the over-sized tires on the truck behind me to crawl up the butt of my Jeep.

Left with no other choice, I was forced to tread ahead until I could find a safe place to turn around and go back for a rescue attempt. I gave it a fifty-fifty chance that I would be able to initiate a U-turn, and still get back in time to save the dog from being struck by one of the zigzagging drivers.

Lots of luck and our Guardian Angels were with the dog and me that day. By the time I pulled the Jeep over to the side of the road and jumped out, the dog was sitting on the double yellow line. His nose was pointed up toward the heavens, and he was slowly rotating his head 180 degrees first one way—then the other. That's when I realized surprise number one; he was blind.

We wouldn't find out until later that his world would always be a dark one, as he was born with almost no eyes. We would also come to call the head rotating I was witnessing for the first time, his *Stevie Wonder* look. Whoops, sorry! There I go, getting ahead of myself.

I ran over to where the dog was sitting, bent down and scooped him up—ignoring the cars as they sped to the right, left, ahead, and behind us. At this point I was thinking for sure I was either going to wind up as road kill or this strange and scared dog was going to take an enormous bite out of me. But, much to my relief, everyone's swerving skills were intact that day and, thanks to the Gods, I didn't get bit either. What did happen, however, was almost surreal.

I will never forget the instant connection I felt with this dog when he wrapped all four-legs around my upper body, laid his head on my shoulder, and melted into my chest. I couldn't help feeling there was some sort of divine intervention going on.

In response to his body-melt, I wrapped my arms around his torso and tightened my grasp, hoping it was enough to reassure him he was now safe and had nothing to fear, including fear itself.

Clinging to each other, we ran back to the safety of my sunny-day Jeep (which is another way of saying there's no enclosed cab, just a cloth bikini top and half doors). When I tried to place him in the passenger's seat, he clung to me like sock-static—refusing to loosen his bear-hugging grip.

I gently stroked his soft white fur and tried to comfort him. "It's going to be OK," I murmured with my mouth pressed up against his ear. He totally ignored my attempt to soothe him and, instead, responded with another one of his *Stevie Wonder* head rotations. That's when I realized surprise number two; this dog's world was not just a dark and obscure one, it was a silent one as well. He was stone cold deaf!

I stood there for a long moment, staring at his rotating head and wondered what to do next. He had no collar. There were a couple of older homes scattered amongst the pine trees a few miles back down the road, but there was no one in the immediate area looking for him.

"Great!" I said out loud to no one in particular, "I've just had a spiritual experience with a lost deaf and blind dog." The dog's only response was another 180-degree head rotation.

"Not that much of a problem though," I continued, despite knowing that I was the only one listening, "Heck no! No problem at all except, of course—the wife!"

One must first understand or, better yet, maybe I should first explain a thing or two. We (the wife and I) already had three Bassett Hounds at home. This meant we were already over the Property Management Association's (POA) mandatory limit of only two dogs.

*Oh well! Whatever!* I thought to myself. *When ya already have three dogs, what difference does it make if you have four? After all, the rules are just as broken with three dogs as they are with four dogs. Right?*

Because I needed to first convince myself, I continued with my foolish efforts to justify bringing this dog home in the hopes I would then be able to convince my wife.

*Besides the already broken rules, four dogs can eat just as cheaply as three...can't they?* Let me tell you the answer to that one turned out to be a big no. And let's not forget the veterinarian's bills either, but there I go again getting ahead of myself.

Back to the subject at hand, *how am I going to con the wife into letting me keep another dog? Especially one who's blind and deaf?* Desperation kicked in—justification moved to the back burner.

With the dog still clinging to me, I suddenly had a great idea. I pulled my trusty cell phone from my front pocket (knowing full well I was calling her from a safe distance) and used one thumb to punch in my home number.

She answered on the second ring. "Hello."

"Ah... hi dear. I've got a situation here."

Ten seconds of silence, then a cautious inquiring response from my loving Snookles (a pet name I gave her many years back, and I suspect it was to get me outta some other mess I had created... but my memory fails me at the moment).

"Ah...and what kind of a situation would that be Alan?" Five more seconds of silence then, "what have you gotten yourself into now?"

I explained myself the best I could while traffic zoomed by, and drivers gawked out their windows at the man and dog standing along side the road, wrapped around each other in a bear-hug.

My fears, much to my relief, were unjustified. Snookles (better known to most folks as Kathi) didn't hesitate this time. She said, "Bring him home, and we'll figure something out."

And with that, the saga of Odd Otis began.

*   *   *

The ride home proved to be both interesting and exciting. The fifty-pound blind, deaf, and frightened dog would have nothing to do with riding in the passenger's seat. It seemed Otis considered the passenger seat to be an entirely unnecessary contraption because my lap would and was doing a fine job—thank you very much. Besides that, he was still not willing to let me escape his bear-hug. I knew I had no other choice but to, somehow, try and drive home with Otis glued to my chest.

Unfortunately, my Jeep is an old one and has a gear shift on the floor that insists on being shifted once in a while (that is if you want to make it home before dark). As you can well imagine, gear shifting proved to be somewhat of a challenge. Fortunately for me, I have long arms so it turned out to be a challenge I was able to meet without dislocating anything.

Steering, however, proved to be somewhat of a different ordeal, as Otis' body was tightly sandwiched in between my chest and the steering wheel. But, the lack of normal steering and shifting capability was painstakingly overcome—my still being here and able to tell this story being proof.

Please do understand that extreme care was used as I vigilantly hugged the right side of the road on the two-mile ride back home. I'm still trying to get over the humiliation of all the pointing and laughing.

The wife claims we were quite a sight when we pulled into our long, graveled driveway.

Otis and I exited the jeep as one—it took several minutes of prying and pulling him from my chest before I was finally able to set him down on the ground. I didn't need to worry about him bolting, as he'd made it obvious he was not going any further than in between my legs.

With Otis now between my bowed-legs instead of glued to my chest, I waddled my way to the garage. I retrieved one of the leashes my Bassets lead *me* around on when the neighbors think I am taking *them* for a walk.

I slid the leash loosely around Otis' neck (remember, he had no collar to attach it to) and, for whatever reason, it seemed to relax him a bit. That's when he decided a reconnaissance mission was in order. With his nose to the ground, he began checking out all the new smells and placing 'dibs' on every plant and bush in our yard.

Once Otis was assured he had total ownership of everything in our front yard, he gave my leg a last quick sniff and an approving sneeze. No longer able to put it off, we headed towards the house, where the real challenges waited—our Bassets (Winchester, Abby, and Lucy) and the wife!

The wife! Oh yes, Kathi, she was the first hurdle to meet us at the door (Otis and I figured we were both in for it). She had already secured the Bassets (hurdles number two, three, and four) in the backyard.

Kathi has always had the uncanny ability to think ahead which, over the years, has put me at a disadvantage on numerous occasions. I have, however, learned to adapt. Having admitted that *I have adapted* means she usually gets what she wants when she wants it and (because she too will be reading my version) she certainly deserves it!

"Oh, he's so cute! Poor little thing!" she said, seeing Otis for the first time.

I knew right then and there we had it made! Poor Otis didn't know though; he's deaf, remember? But, after a few hugs from the wife followed by another, "Oh he's sooo... cute," even Otis realized *things were looking' good bro.*

Relieved, I led Otis into the house and removed the leash.

After giving him several minutes to get acquainted with the new living room smells, we left him to his own demise and went to the back door. It was time to release the Basset herd.

Kathi and I both held our breath as we stood back, and out of the way. I reached over, turned the knob, and swung the back door wide open—nothing happened! Not one Basset Hound came charging through the entryway.

"What the...?"

We peered around the corner of the open door and, much to our surprise, instead of their usual falling all over each other to see who could get through the door first, they were doing a slow belly-crawl across the threshold. Their long, sniffing noses were sticking straight up in the air. It was as plain as white bread—they were already aware that something or someone very strange had dared to enter their territory (house).

In the meantime, Otis was standing in the middle of the living room repeating his *where am I* (Stevie-look). Both he and the Basset herd simultaneously picked up each other's scent (or signal).

All of a sudden, there was a Bassett race to get to the new guy first which, as you can imagine, created an enormous concern as to what was going to happen at the finish line. Hopefully, it was not going to be one of those 'good ole boy' destruction derby type endings.

Kathi and I looked at each other in horror, then chased after the stampeding Bassets.

We knew full well that though the hounds are by nature loveable and harmless, in all of the excitement a possible adverse outcome could be in the making. It would, of course, be something along the lines of them rolling poor Otis over a few times, and scaring the *bejesu*s out of him; which, of course, would result in their upsetting him all over again. Trust me, I did not want to spend another twenty minutes trying to peel a frightened Otis off my chest.

Thankfully, our fears were unwarranted. Otis proved to be a rugged match for Lucy, Winchester, and Abby.

Abby threw in the towel immediately. After giving Otis a couple of quick sniffs, she retreated to her favorite chair. Which, by the way, used to be **my** favorite chair. Lucy said hello with several juicy licks. Winchester (Chester for short) being male himself, sized Otis' *other* end up before giving him a nose-nudge of approval.

Otis took little notice of the two girl Bassets and fell immediately in love with Winchester. One could say it was love at first sight but, seeing how they are both males, let's not say that. We'll just chalk it up to the low warning growls Otis had gotten from both girls, and his being over-anxious to make new friends. The important thing being, the family had bonded.

The sun was beginning to creep behind the pines that made up our skyline, which meant it was dinner time for the three plus one.

Otis, still suspicious of his new surroundings, was on guard for any possible dog food thieves that might be in the near vicinity. His suspicions were not without warrant as our Bassets are chowhounds. As you might already know, a hound-is-a-hound and ours live up to their reputation. This being so, Otis insisted on a personal guard while he ate and that guard, of course, was me.

I used his bowl to lead him into a corner of the kitchen (he had zero tolerance for being pulled or pushed) and then positioned myself so that I was the wall between Otis' bowl and the chowhounds. It seemed to work well, as I heard no complaints or threats being fired at or from Otis.

With dinner done (dogs first, humans second), we searched the linen closet for adequate bedding for Otis. We settled on an old blue blanket but, in the meantime, Otis figured he had already come up with the perfect solution—our leather sofa.

The "no way," battle cry coming out of Kathi was heard around the entire neighborhood.

After a loud argument, a quiet debate, and another loud argument Kathi finally caved and Otis won the leather sofa battle. But that was only because I made the mistake of telling her, "it's a guy thing! I'm a guy, and guys don't have a problem sharing their bed (or sofa) with man's best friend."

Consequently, guess who had to spend the night on the sofa with his new best friend—me!

It also turned out to be somewhat of a long night, as I found Otis to be a bed-hogging snorer. But I suppose it could have been worse, our blanket could have been pink.

# Lost & Found

## Her Version

It was a sight to behold when my husband's Jeep came barreling up our gravel driveway. A large white dog was sitting on his lap with all four of its legs wrapped around his upper body. Alan's head was bobbing from side-to-side as he struggled to peer around the animal's furry head and pointed ears.

Knowing he would bring home a wounded porcupine if I let him, my first thought after receiving his worrisome phone call was, *we already have three dogs; under no circumstances will I let him keep a fourth dog.* And *besides that, we don't know the first thing about caring for a blind dog* (I didn't yet know Otis was also deaf).

Because I know my husband, I also knew his first line of defense for keeping dog number four was going to be, "you told me to bring him home."

Really? What choice did I have? I certainly wasn't going to tell him to put a blind dog back where he found him.

I stood at the living room window overlooking our front yard and watched as Alan paraded Otis around the front yard. He (Otis, not Alan) was lifting his leg and laying claim to anything and everything, including my new garden statues.

Every once in a while, Alan would glance toward the front door with an anxious look. I knew he was waiting for Pandora (me) to pop out of the box he had opened. Because I couldn't help but feel sorry for the both of them, I pasted a smile on my face, opened the door, and waved them in.

Once we got Otis into the house and gave our Basset Hounds the time they needed to settle down, we were able to give Otis a good once-over.    Fortunately, and much to my relief, Alan and I both came to the same conclusion, Otis' owner had been taking good care of him which meant, of course, that they would also be anxious to have him back.

To make sure Alan was clear on the *'they will be anxious to have him back'* point, I reminded him how Otis' clean and recently brushed fur coat, along with his well-fed body was proof positive that someone must be worried and searching for him.

Otis was collarless, so we began planning what the first step to finding his owner was going to be. Thinking he might have somehow managed to slip out of his collar, there was always the possibility his owner had an electronic chip inserted. That being said, we decided to take Otis to a local veterinarian whose office happened to be close to where Alan found him. Maybe they would have a scanner that would detect a microchip. If not, maybe they would recognize him as one of their patients, especially seeing how he had some obvious medical issues.

Because of Otis' insistence on riding only on Alan's lap, and the fact that one needed one-hundred and eighty pounds of man-muscle to shift and steer Alan's macho-jeep, we decided that it would be best if I drove our truck, and Alan and Otis rode shotgun.

During the ride to the veterinarian's office, I realized my husband was going to have a hard time if and when we found Otis' rightful owner. Otis was curled up against Alan's chest with his head lying on his shoulder. Alan's eyes were half-closed as he stroked Otis' backside, and Otis was nuzzling Alan's neck with his nose. Both dog and man were locked into some kind of weird man-dog bonding thing.

After parking the truck, the three of us walked into the veterinarian's office, where everything quickly turned into instant bedlam. We explained to the girls tending the counter how Alan had found this poor deaf and blind dog in the middle of the Skyway. The girls simultaneously gasped, "Oh no!" Then rushed around from behind the counter to hug and coo over Otis.

"Oh, my God! Poor puppy. Is he hurt?" They gushed.

The veterinarian and his assistants came out of their respective exam rooms to see what all the excitement was about.

After a short explanation from us, they squatted down on the floor with Otis and began doing their doctor-thing. They examined his eyes, poked some type of scope down his ears, and pushed on his rib cage— confirming there were no broken bones or other injuries.

Otis took it all in stride. He, in fact, actually seemed to be enjoying all of the attention.

Once the veterinarian and his crew were assured the dog was pain-free, they ran a scanner over his neck and down his backside. "There's no microchip," they said. That's when (much to my dismay) I saw the look of relief on Alan's face. No, truth be told, he lit up like the White House Christmas tree and immediately started asking the vet all kinds of questions about Otis' obvious, and not so obvious, disabilities.

The vet concluded that Otis had been blind since birth, as he hardly had any pupils and that he was, most likely, born deaf as well. He was unable to diagnose Otis' level of hearing loss without extensive tests, but he did wager a guess that Otis was approximately five years old. He also confirmed our earlier findings when he stated, "Otis is in relatively good health. Whoever owns him has been taking good care of him."

As we were leaving the veterinarian's office, I repeated the Vets comment about it being obvious Otis had been well taken care of. A reminder to Alan why we needed to get him back to his rightful and distraught owner as soon as possible.

Alan nodded his head in agreement, but it was a less than

enthusiastic nod. "I know," he said and gently stroked the dog on his lap. After a few more moments of thought, he followed it up with, "we'd be feeling pretty sick inside right now if it was one of our Bassets who'd gotten lost."

I agreed with a firm nod. ""Yes, we would. Which is why you know that we need to do everything we can to find Otis' rightful owner."

Still imagining how he would feel if we lost one of our dogs, Alan suggested we knock on some of the doors in the area close to where he first found Otis. So, with Otis curled up on his lap and still clinging to his chest, we drove off in that direction.

I went door-to-door pushing buzzers while Alan remained in the truck with Otis—letting Alan out of his *sight* was not an option (bad choice of words, but you know what I mean).

I asked the folks who opened their doors if they (or anyone they knew) had a blind and deaf white dog. Despite everyone being genuinely concerned and anxious to help, no one had seen or was aware of a blind white dog living in their neighborhood. They all wished us well, and a few even gave us their blessing before shutting their door.

Having no luck with our door-to-door search (and believe me, I pounded on every single one of them), we finally gave up the search and took Otis back home with us.

What to do next? I decided to call the county's animal shelter and ask if anyone had reported a lost dog that met Otis' description. I dialed the number but was only able to leave a message. It was a Friday evening, and past 5 p.m., so the office was closed until Monday.

It was getting dark and everybody was hungry by this time, so we decided to postpone our search until the next day.

What to call him? We didn't know at the time his name was Otis, and we wanted to call him something other than blind-dog. We bantered names back and forth before finally settling on 'Mr. Magoo,' a blind animated character we both grew up watching on Saturday morning cartoons. We figured we didn't need to worry about confusing poor lost Otis with a *second* name—he's deaf, so he had no clue he had ever had a *first* name. To avoid any confusion, however, and for this story's sake, I will continue to call Otis 'Otis,' though at the time, we were actually calling him Mr. Magoo.

I was concerned about bedding Otis down with the Bassets, as I did not yet trust this odd dog around our over-loveable and sometimes annoying hounds. We have a sunroom just off of our living room, and I felt it was the perfect and safest place for Otis. It would separate him from the hounds and, in case he was a barker, put him out of earshot of the neighbors.

On the other hand, Alan was afraid Otis would be scared if we isolated him in the sunroom, so he thought it would be best if he and Otis slept together on the sofa. I put up a fuss at first, but only because the leather sofa was the only stick of furniture I had left that wasn't covered with dog slobber. In the end, however, I caved—but only because I knew if I didn't, Alan would be up and down all night checking on Otis' wellbeing. At least the sofa was a solution that offered the Bassets and I a better chance at getting some decent *zzzs*. I knew Alan and Otis' sleep time was destined to be minimal. How much shut-eye can an Australian Shepherd and a hundred-and-eighty-pound, full-grown man get while sleeping together on a sofa? My guess—not much.

As it turned out, I was right. They both did more dozing than sleeping. Alan accused Otis of snoring all night, but who knows better than me that poor 'ole Otis was probably just trying to get even.

The next morning, I got up early and dug my camera out of the back of the closet. I took several pictures of Otis and downloaded them onto my computer. With Alan's half-hearted help, we designed a *Lost & Found* poster. He didn't want me to advertise the fact that Otis was blind and deaf. He was sure that if someone other than the actual owner had that information, they would try and claim him as theirs. No! I have no idea why he thought that!

Alan reluctantly took the finished posters, got into his Jeep, and drove around tacking up Otis' picture on the walls of all of our small community's hot spots: Jackie's Diner, the post office, the grocery store and Whisker Pines Pet Shop (whose owner insisted on giving Otis a new collar—free of charge). I love our small mountain community.

After accomplishing his assigned task, my husband drove home—where he let it be known, with guilt-free relief, how there was nothing more he could do to try and find Otis' owner. He then bent down and hugged Otis, rolled him over on his back, and gave him a good 'ole belly rub.

I remember thinking for the second time that Alan was not going to have an easy time of it if and when we found Otis' rightful owner.

As the weekend wore on, I have to admit that even I was finding it hard not to become too fond of Otis. I had to continually remind myself there were two good reasons not to get too attached: One, Otis' rightful owner may very well call any minute: Two, we already had three Basset Hounds, and the last thing we needed was another dog.

Alan and Otis did not try to hide the fact that they were both totally silly over each other. Otis followed Alan everywhere and was constantly begging for lap time. Evidently, nobody told this oversized Australian Shepherd mix he was too big to be a lapdog. On the other hand, Alan couldn't seem to be in the same room with Otis without petting or doting on him.

For the next two days (Saturday and Sunday), I saw the anxious look on Alan's face every time the phone rang, and then the look of relief when he realized it wasn't the phone call he was dreading. I couldn't help but fear my husband's heart was going to be broken heart if someone came to claim Otis.

When Sunday night finally rolled around with still no phone call from Otis' rightful owner, Alan accelerated past being 'hopeful' and concluded that Otis was going to remain unclaimed. He began making all kinds of plans on what we needed to do to keep and care for this special needs dog (by this time, I pretty much knew that our not keeping an unclaimed Otis was no longer an option).

"Okay," he said, squatting down on the floor next to Otis. "We'll call Dr. Colyer (our veterinarian) in the morning and take Otis in for a checkup. We need to have his eyes and ears examined, and we'll see about getting him whatever shots he needs too."

Over the weekend, Otis' not being neutered had begun to cause problems with Winchester. Lucy and Abby were able to dodge poor blind Otis with no problem. They both let him know, under no uncertain terms, his perseverance was going to get him nowhere. Chester, however, is a three-year-old pup; he'll pretty much put up with anything as long as you're willing to play with him. But even he was beginning to lose patience with Otis' playfulness.

"We'll talk to Dr. Colyer about getting Otis fixed too," Alan said. Otis gave his approval by way of a wet tongue across the side of Alan's face, removing any doubt we might have had about the dog's inability to hear.

Alan was so excited about the prospect of keeping Otis that I had to remind him again how the Animal Control Office had been closed all weekend. Anyone needing to call about a lost dog had to wait until the following day (Monday). But Alan's selective hearing kicked in, and he either chose not to hear or pretended not to hear my warning—either way, he totally ignored me.

*   *   *

Monday morning finally rolled around and sure enough, it was only a couple of minutes past eight o'clock when our telephone rang.

I usually love it when I prove my husband wrong—but not this time. A lady named Tina was on the other end of the line claiming to be Otis' owner.

"I think you have my dog," she said. "He's a white, blind, and deaf Australian Shepherd. His name is Otis, and he escaped from my backyard last Friday."

My heart sank. "Yep, that pretty much describes the dog we found," I said. I figured the odds of two deaf and blind Australian Shepherds being lost last Friday was one in ten million, or maybe even a zillion. I gave her our address, and she assured me she would be there shortly to pick him up.

Alan was busying himself with the pooper-scooper in the backyard when I gave him the news. His face fell, and though he tried to look away from me, I saw his eyes fill with tears. I knew he was upset. I felt sick inside. He made the mistake of getting attached to this dog, and now he didn't want to give him back. At the same time, however, he knew Otis rightfully belonged to his original owner.

I tried to console my husband with a reminder of how it was apparent Otis had been well taken care of and how if we lost one of our Bassets, we would certainly want them back. Though he nodded his head in agreement, I knew he was heartbroken.

"I don't want to be rude," he said in a hoarse whisper. "So, when she comes to get Otis, I'm going to get in my Jeep and leave. I don't want to be here when she drives off with him."

I assured him I understood, trying to keep my own tears from welling up and spilling down the sides of my face.

Twenty minutes later, a relieved Tina showed up at our front door. She was a short nervous little lady with huge brown eyes framed in black-rimmed glasses. She looked to be in her early fifties. Her dark brown hair was shoulder length and highlighted with thick strands of natural gray. She wore a loose-fitting dress that hung about three inches below her knees and a pair of old tennis shoes with mismatched socks.

There was another woman with her; she identified herself as Tina's caretaker. She was a pleasant, much younger woman who was seemingly in control of whatever health issues were going on with Tina.

I invited them both in, and Tina immediately began thanking me for finding Otis. Her voice shook as she fought back tears, and told me how worried and upset she had been the entire weekend.

Her caretaker assured me Tina had cried and cried.

I couldn't help myself—I immediately like this offbeat little lady who came to claim Otis. She was sweet and soft-spoken. The dark circles under her eyes told of sleepless nights—deep worry-lines had sunk into her forehead. My heart went out to her.

I explained to Tina that it was Alan, not me, who found Otis. I shared with her the story of how Alan had saved Otis from the middle of the road on the Skyway. And how the two of them had pulled into our driveway wrapped around each other in an octopus' stronghold.

I went on to tell her how Alan had spent the weekend sleeping with Otis on the sofa because he didn't want Otis to be afraid in a strange place. Unable to stop myself, I continued sharing with Tina how quickly our Bassets had accepted Otis and how they taught him to use the doggie door to the backyard.

In my hurry to reassure her that she needn't have worried—I went even further and told her how Alan had been standing guard over Otis and his dinner.

"And, it was the funniest thing to watch my husband trying to play his computer game with a fifty-pound Australian Shepherd on his lap," I said, relieved by the warm smile my blathering had finally placed on Tina's face. "Otis has been in good hands and well-taken care. I promise you he has not been mistreated in any way, shape, or form."

Tina and Otis greeted each other heartily. Lots of licks and hugs and kisses, but the reunion took its toll on Otis. Shortly thereafter, he plopped down on the kitchen floor and took a nap (I say 'plopped' because Otis doesn't lay down like a normal dog, he deflates and then free falls to the floor).

I didn't ask Tina why Otis wasn't tagged and collared. Obviously, this delightful, unconventional little lady was doing her best with whatever resources she did or did not have. I did, however, ask her how she had acquired Otis.

Tina explained that she rescued Otis and his sister, Twiggy (blind but not deaf), right after they were both born. When she learned that (due to their disabilities) the breeder would have to put both Otis and Twiggy down, she knew she could not let that happen. Despite the breeder's warning that the pups were going to be a terrible burden, she scooped them both up and took them home.

Tina went on to explain that she had two more rescued dogs, both Pitbull's. One Pitbull (Sky) was sweet and docile, but the other she said tended to have a mean streak and was cause for concern.

When I asked how Otis had gotten out of her backyard, Tina shook her head and admitted she had no idea. She was fearful that someone had purposely opened the gate. She then shared another story about an altercation with her neighbor and his dislike for Otis. Evidently, there was an escalating barking problem, and she was worried the neighbor might harm Otis. Though she didn't come right out and say it, she hinted he might have been the source of Otis' escape.

Still describing how upset she had been over Otis' disappearance, she shared how (despite her shyness) she had stood up and tearfully revealed her loss of Otis to the members of her Church. "My church," she said, "has been praying for me."

And that—unfortunately—is the moment Alan chose to come bursting through the side door that leads to our garage.

He took the hundred-dollar bill he had in his hand and slapped it down on the breakfast bar in front of Tina. I'll give you a hundred dollars for the dog," he told Tina, his pale face laced with stress. Not waiting for an answer, he turned around and stalked out. Slamming the door behind him.

I was so embarrassed. I wanted to kill him—very slowly. Tying him to an anthill—or something equally torturous crossed my angry mind.

Tina and the caretaker both looked at me in surprise. When I heard the Jeep startup, I frantically began to apologize for my husband's bad behavior. I quickly began describing to Tina how attached Alan had gotten to Otis despite my warnings. "He told me he was going to leave before you got here because he couldn't stand watching someone drive off with Otis," I said.

I went on to explain how, after waiting all weekend for a phone call that didn't come, Alan had convinced himself that no one was going to claim Otis. Continuing my desperate attempt to make amends, I told her his plan to call and schedule Otis an appointment with our veterinarian this morning. "And just yesterday, he went to the pet store and bought Otis a new tag for his collar." I showed Tina the tag hanging around Otis' neck with *Magoo* etched on it.

Tina listened intently to everything I said, then graciously assured me that an apology wasn't necessary. She stared at Otis for a long moment, reached down, and patted him on the head, and then she said the most extraordinary thing, "I think maybe Otis would be better off living here with you and Alan."

"No, no!" I protested in surprise. "Otis is your dog, Tina. That's not right. He belongs to you."

Tina's eyes narrowed. "I'm a Christian. I believe everything happens for a reason and that for whatever reason, Otis and Alan are meant to be together," she said.

At this point, even the caretaker chided in. "Tina, why don't you think about it for a couple of days, and then if you still feel that way, we'll bring Otis back."

I agreed with the caretaker, but Tina wasn't having it.

"I'm fifty-two years old," she said, irritated at being challenged, "and I can make up my own mind."

I didn't know what to say. A lump formed in my throat. I was overjoyed for my husband's sake, but at the same time, I didn't want to take Otis away from this genuinely sweet and kind-hearted lady. But Tina was persistent. She stood steadfast in her belief that there was a spiritual reason for Otis and Alan's chance meeting on the Skyway.

The fruitless debate continued for several more minutes before the caretaker and I both finally conceded. Tina's only request was that she be allowed to come by now and then to visit Otis, and could she also please bring Otis' sister, Twiggy?

Even more astonishing, she refused to take the hundred-dollar bill Alan had left on the bar, even though there was no doubt in my mind she could have used it.

Shortly after that Tina and her caretaker announced it was time for them to go. Tina and I and the caretaker all hugged each other.

Tina hugged and kissed Otis and wrote down her address and phone number. We exchanged goodbyes. I tried not to look at the tears rolling down both of their cheeks when they left. I knew if I did, the tears running down my own cheeks would most likely divert to hysterical sobbing.

A good hour slipped by before I saw the Jeep finally pull into our driveway and my husband walk through the door. Dark glasses hid what I knew were swollen eyes—the corners of his mouth twisted downward.

"Well," he said. If she took the dog and left the hundred dollars, she truly cares about him, which is a good thing. If she took the hundred dollars and left the dog, then she truly doesn't care about him, and we'll keep him—and that's a good thing."

I stared back at him for a long moment before answering. "Well…how about this for caring about the dog? She left the hundred dollars and the dog."

Alan stared at in stunned silence.

"You're kidding," he finally said.

"No. I'm not. She left the hundred dollars and the dog."

The angst on his face melted. "Oh my God," he said, looking down at his feet. A deafening silence filled the room. "I bullied her into letting me keep Otis, and that's not right."

He paced back and forth for several minutes before finally asking, "Did you get her address?"

I confirmed that I had.

"I have to go talk to her," he said, more to himself than to me, "Otis is her dog, and I had no right to bully her into giving him to me."

Without saying a word, I handed Alan the address Tina left on the breakfast bar.

"What in the world was I thinking?" he said, continuing to chastise himself as he exited out the front door. He jumped into his Jeep and took off down the road—engine roaring. I had no idea what was going to happen next.

*   *   *

I paced and waited, and waited and paced. Then I paced some more. The long minutes turned into hours and continued to tick by slower and slower.

Finally, I heard the man-jeep coming down the road. I grabbed a cold beer from the refrigerator, figuring either Alan or I would need it, and Otis and I went outside to greet him.

Though I was dying to ask him what happened, I gritted my teeth and waited impatiently as he slowly got out of the man-jeep—accepted the cold beer and sat down on the steps leading to our front door. He took a deep breath, popped open the bottle, put an arm around Otis' neck, and took a long, irritating swig.

"Tina was surprised when she opened the door and saw me standing there," he finally said. "I apologized profusely, but she was insistent that no apology was necessary and invited me in."

He told me how they talked about Otis, Twiggy, the pit bulls, the problem neighbor, and most importantly, what was best for Otis. They shared their spiritual convictions with each other and Tina's belief in divine intervention. Last but not least, Tina revealed to Alan how she had been involved in a tragic auto accident when she was only nineteen years old and had long since struggled with significant health issues. She explained how Otis' unconditional love had taught her the importance of patience and kindness over the years. She finished by saying, "I feel the time has come for me to forward my fur-angel on to the next person."

The end result of their conversation being—Otis would continue to live with us, and we had just made a new and wonderful friend named Tina.

I was relieved my husband had made things right with Tina. I was happy he was happy and that we were going to be able to keep Otis after all, and I honestly think Tina was right when she said, "I believe everything happens for a reason." The reason (of course) remains to be seen, but deep down, I too am confident that Otis and Alan are destined to start a new adventure together. There is, however, one more thing that remains to be seen and that is, "what is my part in this new adventure going to be?"

Even though I have to admit that I have also grown attached to this very odd dog, it has still not kept the wiser part of my inner self from silently crying out "OMG…four frigging dogs!"

*I may not see you eye-to-eye,*
*I may not hear you ear-to-ear,*
*But I see and hear you heart-to-heart*

# Snoozing on the leather sofa.....

# Two Weeks Later

# Musical Chairs

*As told by Alan Hiatt*

*Scratch a dog and you will find a permanent job*
*~Franklin P Jones*

These last two weeks have been a time of adjustment for not only Otis but for Kathi and me as well…. and, of course, the Bassets.

Out of all of the hounds, poor Abby got the worst end of it. Especially when you take into account that she was still trying to adjust to Winchester, whom we had adopted the year before. Her still trying to adjust after a year might sound strange but if you knew Winchester you would completely understand. There's a reason that we eventually changed his nickname from "Chester" to "Pester".

We rescued Abby from a puppy mill when she was seven months old where, unfortunately, she had not been properly socialized. To this day she suffers because of the neglect—she is shy and skittish. Consequently, Otis's attempts to woo Abby equaled total chaos. At least, that is, until she finally realized that this strange new dog (who was always running into walls and furniture) couldn't find his way out of a dog food bag, let alone have any success at courting her.

Lucy, on the other hand, let Otis know right up front that she did not appreciate his attempts to *woo* her. Shortly thereafter she and Otis seemed to have an understanding of the ways, and I think that's when Otis decided he liked Winchester best anyways.

True to the color of her fur (a red head) Lucy is our *little rascal*

Basset. She is the smartest of the three and has an uncanny knack for getting into mischief. She steals and chews up all unguarded pairs of eyeglasses, remotes, and toilet paper. As mind-boggling as it sounds she not only pins it on Winchester, but has even figured out a way to convince Winchester he did it. We know this because if we ask, "who did this (in spite of the piece of toilet paper still stuck to Lucy's lip)?" Winchester lowers his head and whines. With this being said, we can't help but think Lucy was more than happy to welcome another male to pin her dirty deeds on.

Lucy being Lucy, however, is not all bad. She has since granted Otis permission to clean her eyes and ears, but only if she happens to be in the mood!

Let's get back to my favorite chair—that has since become Abby's favorite chair and is, therefore, no longer mine. I had bought an extra-large recliner that was capable of seating both Kathi and me whenever we wanted to cozy-up, but we never really had a chance to try it out before Abby took it over. Back then Chester would sometimes risk a butt-nip and tease poor Abby just so he could commandeer her chair….that used to be mine. He would stretch his long body across the seat and rest his head on one of the arms which, of course, blocked her from jumping up.

Otis, on the other hand, was a different story. He decided that the oversized recliner, the green recliner-rocker, AND the sofa would all work for him. Poor Otis. Time to learn the rules.

Musical chairs took place for a couple of days until everyone learned the ground rules, especially Otis. Even Lucy got in on the action by sneaking in a chair-steal now and then.

When the dust finally settled, Abby had dibs on my extra-large recliner, but had decided to share it with Lucy—if she happened to be in a sharing mood. Chester had the green rocker-recliner and Otis had the leather sofa. We, humans, squeezed in where ever and whenever there might be a little bit of extra room. I have since become partial to the floor and a pillow that Kathi got for me to sit on because, evidently, the riveted back pockets on my jeans will wear out the carpet.

Does anyone have any idea why a deaf dog barks? Thought not. Did I tell you Otis barks? My Bassets will bark to get a treat and whatever else they think they might want. They know if they create enough of a commotion the master (me) will surely come running and will give them exactly what they are barking for. My Bassets must be saying, "We've trained the master well, have we not?"

The explanation for Otis' barking must be because he senses the bark within him, and how it always prompts me to come running—like a well-trained master—every time! The end result always being the same, he then gets what he wants. Logical. Gosh, all I had to do was put in on paper and it became as clear as the long white nose on Otis's face.

One of Otis' favorite pastimes, besides napping, is watching TV and eating popcorn with me. I know…I know… Otis is blind how can he watch TV? Remember the inner sense that he has for barking? Well, it seems to work for TV watching too. I'm trying to decide what Otis likes best; westerns, dramas, sci-fi, action, or is it popcorn? My vote is the popcorn.

Popcorn gets tossed to all the dogs and often lands on the carpet and, eventually, in all four corners of the room. For obvious survival reasons we, or the pack I should say (I'm an honorary member), only do this when the wife's not home. Kathi just wouldn't understand nor would she tolerate popcorn thrown all over the living room. Wives and mothers can be like that, as all of us men know.

Another oddity about Otis, ah oh…Odd Otis? That sounds better than *Ottie-Toddie* doesn't it? That's what Kathi is starting to call Otis and we guys think that it sounds way too girlie. Odd Otis sounds like a cool guy name so I'm going with it.

Anyway, Odd Otis likes to try and carry his food bowl around in his mouth. We're guessing the reason he does this is because he had measurable competition at his old home, and having one's bowl under one's nose was the safest and best way to protect such a valuable possession.

Because our Bassets are hounds (I think I mentioned that earlier) we have Basset Hound bowls. These bowls are designed so that the Bassets' exceptionally long ears don't get into their food and they don't wind up eating their own ears. This being the case, the sides of the bowls have a design that just won't allow Odd Otis to get a good grab with his teeth, and a good grab is needed to carry a bowl. To further Odd Otis' frustration the bowls are also made of stainless steel, thus making it another hardship in the art of bowl carrying. I would get Odd Otis a better carrying bowl, but dog food dumped on the kitchen floor would probably get Odd Otis and I both into a bunch of trouble with you know who.

Night time brings bedtime for all. Preparations must be made and, again, routines must be established. We've come to realize that all dogs seem to love routines, no matter what might be involved. Though he is deaf and blind Odd Otis is no exception to this doggie rule.

For now, Odd Otis's sleeping quarters are in the sunroom. Only because he likes to bark and get everybody out of bed in the middle of the night for some belly scratching and playtime. I guess if you're blind and deaf, any time of the day or night is a good time to play and bark, and get your belly scratched. How is he to know there is an *a.m.-p.m.*?

Consequently, until this dilemma is solved, Odd Otis must stay banished to the sunroom at night—which also happens to be the room furthest from our bedroom. This might sound cruel but it is not. He has his own doggie pillow, his own heater, and in the summer time his own air conditioner. He even has access to a second leather sofa, when he feels the need. Remember... Odd Otis likes leather.

We try to understand Odd Otis as best we can and we accommodate him as much as we can. Though Odd Otis sleeps by himself in the sunroom, we are hoping that at some point we can get him to sleep with the Bassets in my wife's office (which, by the way, Kathi sarcastically refers to as the 'kennel').

Until that time comes, dog beds (with 2-blankets each) are laid down in both rooms, along with a bowl of water and a couple of toys. Truth be known, we have actually purchased eight of these extra-large dog beds. Four for bedtime, and four for sunning on the deck. They are, of course, for the convenience of the dogs. Though I admit that I have, on occasion, slept on them myself.

"Why?" you ask. Because on stormy windy nights it's the only way I'm able to comfort our Basset, Lucy. She begins to whimper and shake because she thinks that the *wind monster* is after her, or the *lightning monster*, or the *thunder monster*, or the *pine cone falling on the roof monster.*

I have only had to settle in for the night with Odd Otis twice. His first night with us; and then again after he visited the veterinarian's office and no longer wanted to show the girl dogs (or Winchester) how much he *loved* them. He was feeling sorry for himself that particular night. Which is why I saw fit to comfort him in his hour of need, and to comfort myself as well since I'm the one who had to ante up for the vet's bill.

As one can see adjustments and oddities have been made and they continue to be made. Even with us human types. Our routines for bedding down for the night and getting up in the mornings has changed for both Kathi and I.

The Bassets sleep behind the closed French doors leading to Kathi's office, which is also the room that houses the dog door leading to the backyard's poop area. This means Odd Otis has no free access to the outside until after we let the Bassets in the next morning. And believe me, no one wants Basset vs Otis chaos first thing in the morning.

The agreed upon rules are that whoever gets up first is who is stuck with taking Odd Otis for a potty-walk in the front yard. As you might recall, we live in a mountain community where winter mornings are icy and cold. While walking Odd Otis in your robe and slippers, don't forget to pick up the morning paper. If it's a Friday, don't forget to drag the garbage can down to the end of the gravel driveway and, whatever you do, don't step onto the icy asphalt when you reach the bottom. Kathi did that once and had the neighborhood been awake, they would have known that she owns a pair of Scooby-Doo panties....a Christmas present from our granddaughter.

Odd Otis' potty-walk is immediately followed by straightening up and picking up whatever mess he has created in the sun room… when he was supposed to be sleeping. "The mess" is a direct result of Odd Otis's spending the night trying to find his way around. Consequently, he nose-bumps and sometimes knocks over a variety of dirt filled pots, his water bowl, garden statues, and/or a hodgepodge of other decorative items that Kathi has filled the sunroom with.

He is, however, getting better at finding his way around. He now knows how to use one of the sunroom's patio chairs as a step-up to the top of the patio table, where he curls up into a ball and takes a short snooze. Don't ask me… I have no clue why in Odd Otis' head a cold and slippery glass table top makes a good bed.

On the other hand, he who thinks he has been fortunate enough to stay in bed now has to get up and make the bed, open the blinds, put away the remotes, rinse out the ice cream bowls (our favorite night time snack) and Kathi's water glass...and put away any other miscellaneous items from the night before.

Next, the second waker-upper must fling open the French doors leading to Kathi's office. The Bassets, of course, are no longer asleep. They are now whining, barking, and pawing at the door. Stand back second waker-upper, because this is when Lucy, Chester, and Abby *bolt* through the door. Oh yes, and because he is back from his morning potty-walk, Odd Otis is coming from the other direction at the same time.

While Odd Otis and the hounds are exchanging excited morning greetings, second waker-upper must gather up the dog toys and fold and put away the numerous blankets Otis and the hounds sleep with. Can't let them get cold at night, even though they have fur coats and their own propane stove. If it's Thursday, peel the covers off the dog pillows and throw them, the numerous blankets, and any stinky dog toys into the washer. This is usually all being done while you're still half asleep and blurry-eyed. Now it's "Did I brush my teeth yet or was that yesterday?" Another day has begun!

Doggie *cookie time* (aka: breakfast) consists of two good doggie treats, followed by one more really good treat, and then finished off with a really, really, good treat. The hounds have been participating in this morning ritual since they were little pups, but Odd Otis is a new member of the breakfast club. At first, he hung back and was hesitant. But a treat is a treat and if a guy is to score, ya' gotta get in there and stand your ground. Odd Otis being Odd Otis has since learned how to bully his way to the head of the line—he's taller than the short-legged Bassets and can step over them.

Everyone is aware of the rules. If you drop your cookies it's fair game. Me being a softy I always make sure that the mandatory amount is given to each, and if one or two of them happen to score a 'drop', it's a bonus.

After a hearty breakfast, Odd Otis likes to continue to hang around the kitchen for a while. He sits or lays down, turns on his perked-ears radar, and then waits for one of those 'drops'. Which, of course, never happens because cookie time is over! I'm sure he's going to catch on sooner or later. It's only been two weeks and a day. When he does finally catch on, I'm sure he'll forego this ritual and will instead join in on the run-around-the-house game with the rest of the pack.

After *cookie time*, it's naptime. You have to understand getting up in the morning, finding the perfect place to poop outside, eating a "doggie" breakfast and then chasing each other around the house for twenty minutes is exhausting…so of course, a nap is in order.

Odd Otis goes to *his* leather sofa for some shut eye while the others find their chair of choice. In the meantime, I'm still trying to decide whether or not I've already brushed my teeth. "What the heck!" I say to Kathi "Brushing twice can't hurt, but not brushing at all can." So I'm off to the bathroom to brush my teeth…most likely for the second time that morning.

Remember that odd inner sense that Odd Otis has for barking and TV watching? Well, he also has an inner sensory clock. I swear you can set your watch by Odd Otis because he knows exactly when his dinner time is. Every evening he goes to the kitchen, barks a couple of times, and then shows me where the doggie dinner bowls are…just in case I might have forgotten. We have a large assortment of different dog foods in the cupboard. I suspect that we have enough by now to start our own pet store. Odd Otis is picky. He loves treats, but as soon as I pour dog food into his bowl his nose goes straight up in the air and he refuses to eat it. Now if I hand-feed him, he at least tolerates the flavors and textures. So much for the printing on the bag that guaranteed me my dog will surely love the enclosed crunchy, delicious tidbits. There must be some small print somewhere that says *except for Odd Otis*.

Did I mention that Odd Otis likes shrimp? Did I mention that Odd Otis likes steak, pork chops, chicken, hamburger, fresh fish, and carrots? Ah ha…gott'cha didn't I? "Carrots?" you say. Yes, he loves them. We're still trying to figure out why he's partial to rabbit food, but we don't expect any success as we have made little headway in trying to figure out what kind of dog food he likes. I was down at the pet store the other day and, luckily, I've still got about a dozen more brands and flavors to choose from.

Odd Otis is making progress. He is adjusting to us and us to him. In fact, I am happy to report that a routine is finally beginning to be established and, for the most part, is now pretty repetitious. This is especially comforting to us humans who happen to both be September born, over-organized Virgos. Oh yes, did I mention that Abby is also a Virgo? One would think with three Virgos we would have a pristine household, right? Wrong!

Our home is often referred to as the 'doghouse' when it comes time to vacuum up the dog hair, wash the dog blankets, pick up the doggy toys, remove sticky dog slobber from the furniture, and mop the muddy paw prints off the laminate floors. I'm sure you've guessed that it's the wife again with that hurtful insult. She just doesn't understand that it takes a lot of effort to get those toys scattered about and those blankets smelling just right…her failure to understand has Odd Otis and the Bassets (and me) all baffled. The hounds care the most. Hours and hours of work getting things to smell just right, and scattered just right…ruined in one afternoon! Unbelievable!

Odd Otis appears to be the only patient one. His having to shed some more fur on the carpet, muck up the blankets again, drag out more toys, and restock the floor with fresh paw prints seems to not be a problem for him. In fact, I think he enjoys it. After all, he needs to have something to do in between nap time and dinner.

So, all's quite at *Home Sweet Home*. I admit it's been trying at times but in the end, it's been a good couple of weeks. Odd Otis seems to be happy and has pretty much settled in. Routines have been somewhat established for now and all four dogs and both humans seem to kind-of-sort-of know their place. Life is Good......so far!

# Making Friends

*I would rather walk with a friend in the dark, than alone in the light*
*~Helen Keller*

*My Basset sister, Lucy, likes to tell me jokes....*

*I can't hear her, but her breath tickles my ear, so I laugh really loud!*

*1,2,3... I like to play Hide & Seek...*

*But, everyone always finds me. I wonder why!*

*You might be surprised to know that I can do lots of things that other dogs do.*

*When you tap my nose twice, I know you are asking me to sit!*

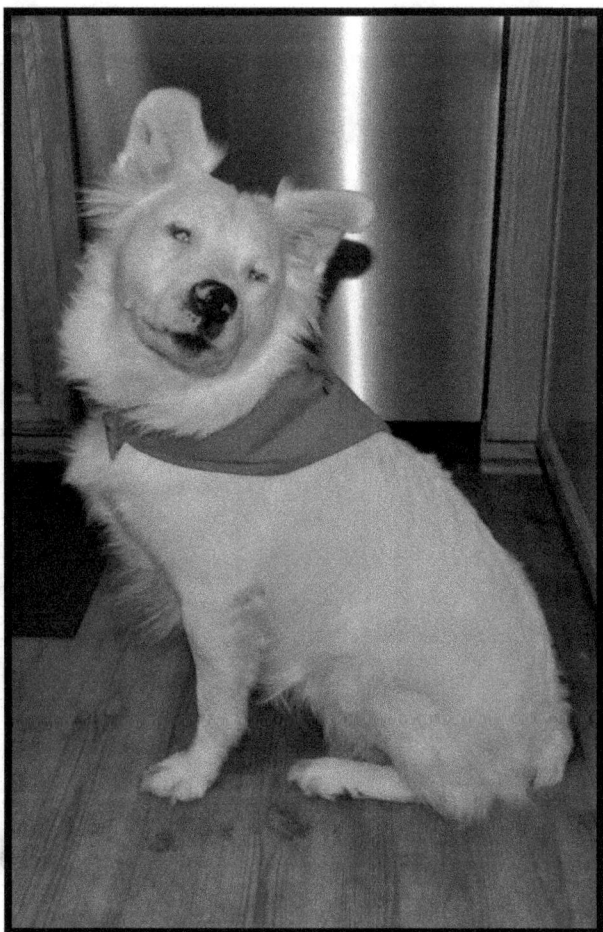

*When you tap my shoulder twice, I will shake your paw (hand)!*

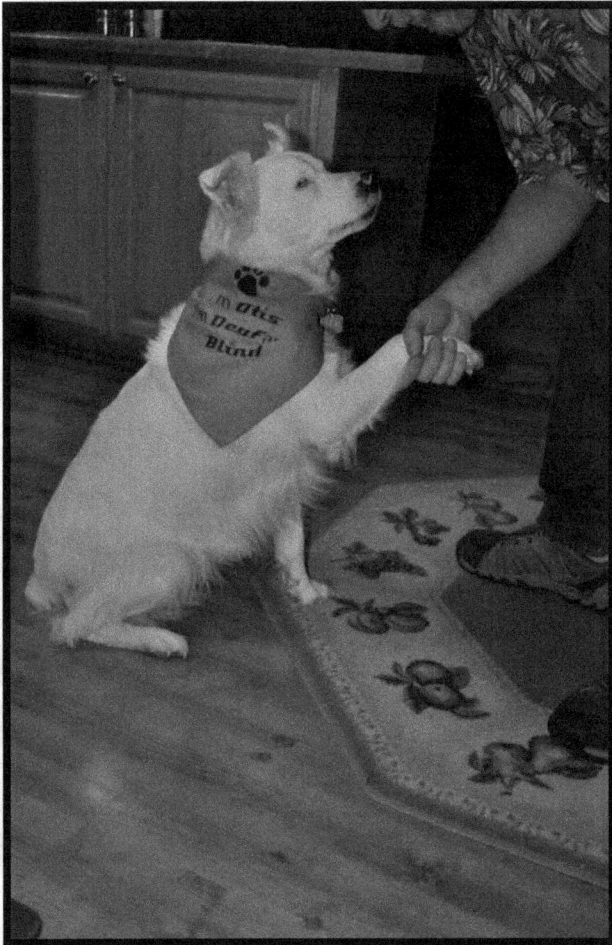

*I can't see, but I can find the doggie door to go do my outside business.*

# The Great Escape

*As told by Kathi Hiatt*

Odd Otis was with us for about a week when he made what Alan calls his attempted *Great Escape.*

We are still mystified as to why because the food is great, the TV is big, and we would like to think that we give good belly rubs. My guess is Odd Otis didn't actually try to escape. I don't think dogs really understand the concept of escaping or running away. They do, however, understand that whether it be a kitty cat or a great looking fire hydrant there is always something interesting on the other side of a fence.

Our backyard is completely enclosed with a durable four foot chain-link fence, so you can imagine my surprise when I went outside and found Odd Otis sniffing at something amongst the pine needles—in the neighbor's yard. Which is, of course, on the other side of the fence. Stunned and scratching my head in bewilderment I scanned the yard trying to figure out what and how it had happened.

There was just no way!

After unlocking the cyclone gate (yes, it was locked) and leading Odd Otis back into our yard, I walked the parameter of our fenced yard looking for a possible escape route. There were no freshly dug holes and every single chain link was intact. Now I was really baffled. I decided I needed a second opinion so, I hollered for Alan to come and help me solve the mystery of Otis's great escape.

He too walked the parameter of our yard, and then admitted that he was as mystified as I was. "Maybe there's an underground tunnel somewhere with a camouflaged entrance and exit," he said.

I actually gave his 'maybe' five solid seconds of serious consideration before putting the *kibosh* on his crazy thinking...proof that one or both of us must finally be losing it.


The fence was way too high for the dogs to jump over and, besides that, Odd Otis can't see so he's incapable of determining how high or low a fence is. In his world, a four-foot fence and a twelve-foot wall are one and the same.

How Odd Otis managed to get out of the yard without the Bassets in tow was also baffling. Those Hounds certainly would never have allowed him to go exploring without their help. We were in a perplexing dilemma and, therefore, had no choice but to resort back to crazy thinking. Was Odd Otis an alien with teleporting skills, or was he capable of some sort of time travel, or was it the camouflaged tunnel thing after all? Nothing made any sense.

Beyond our fence line is a heavily forested green belt with free roaming lions, tigers, and bears. Okay, maybe it's really squirrels, skunks, and raccoons but they can be pretty mean too. We certainly couldn't and wouldn't ban Odd Otis from the back yard, but we also had to keep him from an accidental meet and greet with a forest critter. This meant we had no other choice except to find Houdini-Odd Otis's escape route.

We sat down on the steps of the deck, determined to stay there until we either discovered how he was getting out or we were covered with cobwebs...whichever came first.

Fortunately, we didn't have to wait long. It was only a matter of minutes before Odd Otis began to zigzag back and forth across the yard. A ploy he was using to map out where the fence line was. Next, he used his nose to follow the mapped line—sniffing his way down the side of the enclosure until he reached the locked cyclone gate.

We watched in amazement as Odd Otis, a fifty pound Australian Shepherd, managed to reduce his entire body mass (which was mostly fur) to a mere five inches wide—two inches smaller than the width of this book—by turning his head sideways and squeezing between the hinged side of the gate and the edge of the house.

We couldn't believe what we were seeing!

This explained why the Bassets weren't with him. There was no way their broad chests and pot bellies would have fit through a five-inch gap or, for that matter, a fifteen-inch gap. I unlocked the gate and, once again, led Odd Otis back into his own yard. This time, I secured him in the house while Alan figured out how he was going to block any future escape attempts by Odd Otis.

After an hour or so of pondering, hammering, and cursing, Alan figured it out. Odd Otis was, once again, secured inside the safety of his new backyard.

# The Great Escape.........

# Three Months Later

# "Bumper" Marks

*As told by Alan Hiatt*

*My dog's not spoiled, I'm well trained*

It's been a good three months and the dust is finally beginning to settle. Everyone's routines have become more established and...well, routine. There are, however, a few new routines and rituals that have popped up here-and-there. Odd Otis's being on my lap every morning while I'm paying bills has become one of them.

Why he's not sitting on my lap right now and trying to help me type is only because he's already spent a good hour helping me with my on-line bill paying. Consequently, he's pooped himself out and is now sleeping in the one and only extra chair in my office. And, it's beginning to look as though Odd Otis has put his claim on that chair too. It's leather and as we **all** know by now, Odd Otis is partial to leather. I think it's maybe because of his long fur. The cool leather must keep him cooler than my lap does and, believe me, I am thankful for that. Otherwise, I'm afraid I might have had to wear Odd Otis all day.

Odd Otis has established two other habits and of the two, one is somewhat baffling. When he's planted in my lap and it's apparent to all that he is happy and content, he will begin to yawn—repeatedly—over and over again. It's a bit strange, but it's a really wide yawn that also gives me an opportunity to check out his teeth. Thankfully, I am happy to report they are in fine shape as my vet charges more for Odd Otis's dental work than my dentist, Dr. Pryde, does for me. If Odd

Otis happens to need any future dental work, I'm actually considering switching him over to Dr. Pryde.

Odd Otis's other habit occurs when he is snuggled up on one of our laps and start's moaning with pleasure. I mean to tell you…he gets passionately loud. In certain situations this can be somewhat uncomfortable—like when we have friends over, or holiday party guests, or my wife's mother. So far, everyone has either laughed or pretended like they hadn't noticed—except my wife's mother. She rolls her eyes and mumbles something that sounds a whole lot like, "for God's sake, get that dog a girlfriend."

I don't expect or want Odd Otis to change any of his strange habits. These are all the things that make Odd Otis odd…but it certainly doesn't make it any less embarrassing in mixed company.

The dog-day afternoons around our house mostly consist of napping and some playtime. Odd Otis is the underdog when it comes to playing as he, for obvious reasons, is considered the weak link in the dog pack. I'm ashamed to say that the Bassets take advantage of his weaknesses, but dogs will be dogs and all's fair in love, war, and doggie playtime.

Doggie playtime is defined as running around the house at full speed and exiting and entering whatever doggie door is open, and happens to be the closet—we have three doggie doors. It's exceptionally funny to watch three full-sized hounds trying to get through a doggie door at the same time! Odd Otis is always in the rear so it works to his advantage, even though he doesn't know it.

Odd Otis's eating habits have improved considerably and my empty wallet can prove it. Little did we know that not only did Odd Otis not have a lack of appetite, he was also not a picky eater.

As you might recall, his first home had been somewhat of a challenge because one of the Pitbull Terriers that lived with him had a big appetite, and an occasional mean streak. Tina has since shared with us how Odd Otis would try and protect his food by carrying his bowl around between his teeth and hiding it in one of his secret spots—which was either under his blanket, or covered up with a piece of paper or whatever else he found lying on the floor.

We are guessing that when he first came to live with us he must have decided our Bassets were just as scary as the Pitbull. But, unfortunately for him, he couldn't get a good hold on his new bowl because of the slippery stainless steel sides. And, to make matters worse, there was nothing lying around on the floor to cover his new bowl up with (remember, we are obsessive neat freaks). This meant that the only safe eating place was from my hand.

Fortunately, Odd Otis has since learned that his Basset-fears were only partially justified. Once the Bassets finish their own food, they are too passive in nature to fight for anyone else's. They are, however, not above sneaking around from behind and stealing what's left of someone else's. Having learned this, Odd Otis now eats just as fast as the Bassets….problem solved.

Oh, and since we are on the topic of food, all dogs love to chew on bones, right? Well, kinda. Odd Otis thinks that bones are for one thing and one thing only, and that is to bury them as deep and as fast as he can. Needless to say, it only takes the Bassets all of five seconds to find and dig Odd Otis' bones back up—seeing's how they sat on the deck and watched him bury it.

Because bones are considered good dental tools for keeping your canine's teeth clean, I tried everything; including isolating Odd Otis in the garage. My hope was that if he couldn't smell the Bassets, he would chew instead of bury. No such luck. He was just sure that if he dug long and hard enough on that cement floor, he'd eventually break ground and dig a hole deep enough to bury his bone in. I've reassigned finding the solution to this problem to Kathi.

After dinner and once the dogs are bedded down, Kathi and I go around the house picking up all sorts of doggie paraphernalia; toys, chewed up pine cones, half-eaten beetles, and any other items that require a Kleenex for pick-up because we're unsure if it's dead or alive.

Windex Spray removes the bumper-marks from low-lying windows, mirrors, and glass cabinet doors. Bumper-marks are the marks Odd Otis's nose leaves while navigating throughout the house. His navigational skills are getting better each day though, so we anticipate there will be fewer and fewer bumper-marks in the up and coming months. This, of course, will also mean an up and coming reduction in our Windex expense.

Lastly, hair spray removes the pitch from the laminate flooring that they are all guilty of tracking in on their paws.

Finally! We get to *hit the hay*.

# Neuter Night

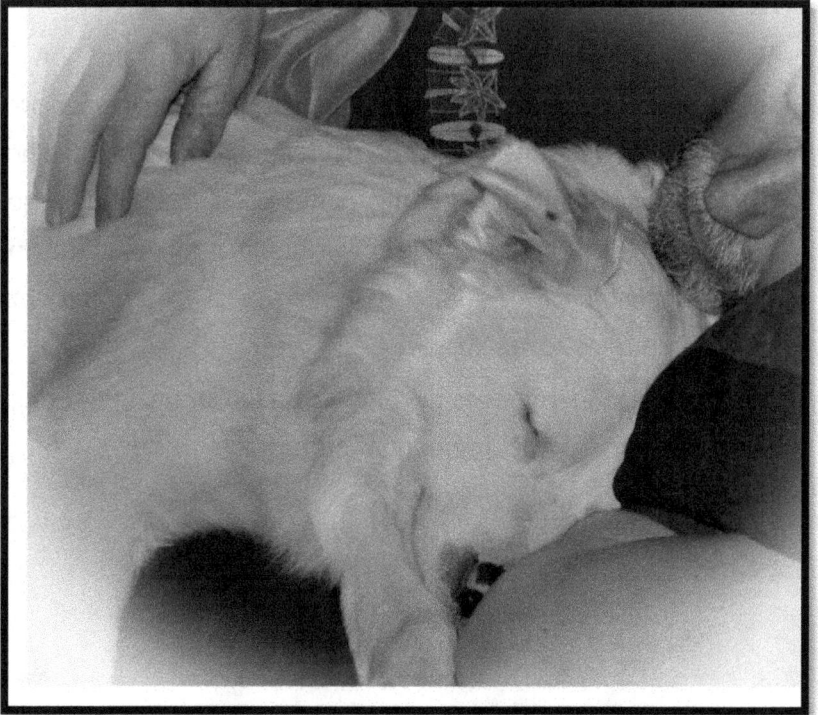

# Odd Otis' Silent Darkness

*By Kathi Hiatt*

*"Put down blind & deaf dogs," is what the breeder said to do*
*But you cried out in protest, then took me home with you*
*You whispered softly in my ear, you saved me from my death*
*I could not hear your words, but felt the tickle of your breath*

*My bowl is never empty, I have a pillow for my head*
*I know that I am safe, for I sleep peaceful in my bed*
*A silver tag and collar, hang loosely around my neck*
*You say that I am yours, on a chip that is high tech*

*When you gently tap my nose, are you asking me to sit?*
*The hug & treat that follows, says to me it's what you meant*
*You have opened up the door, to the silent dark within*
*Now we can communicate, now my being begins*

*You advocate to others; you teach them to be kind*
*To animals like me, who may be deaf or blind*
*You show them how with help, and a little guidance too*
*That though I'm special needs, there's nothing I can't do*

# One Year Later

# The Trickster

*As told by Alan Hiatt*

*After we bring food home from the grocery store they must think we are the greatest hunters ever!* ~Ann Taylor

Over the last year I've tried on several occasions to encourage Odd Otis to go bug (I mean help) Kathi fix breakfast in the morning. But, unfortunately for me his decision early on to be on my lap while I am on my computer has not changed. What has changed is that he no longer climbs up… he now insists that he be picked up and placed squarely on my lap. *Squarely* might be a bad choice of words because poor Odd Otis is just not a good fit. He is too big and, therefore, has problems with his protruding extremities poking out here and there and everywhere. Consequently, about the time I've completed an account transaction and I'm about to hit the *Enter* key, out pops one of Odd Otis' legs and lands on the keyboard. Anyone with any keyboard experience knows what the end result is when this happens. Because I am not easily discouraged, I continue on with my typing. Sometimes I'm using only one hand and at other times I'm using the hunt and peck method; in spite of the fact that when I was in high school I mastered 65 words per minute on a manual typewriter. If you don't know or are not familiar with a manual typewriter, it is completely understandable. It just means that you're not a senior citizen.

Once Odd Otis and I have finished paying the last of the *first of the month's* on-line bills, I like to recite a quick silent prayer in the hopes that it all went to the right place. If not, I am sure that our creditors will let me know and I am equally sure that they will understand why the car payment went to the water company, and the water company's money went to the garbage man. With Odd Otis on my lap, it's always a wait and see.

After I log off and before I remove Odd Otis from my lap, he insists on a belly rub. I have not yet been able to predetermine the contortionist moves Odd Otis uses to get into position, but I'm getting close. It's something like a twist, followed by a turn, another turn, and then a final flip...Presto! Odd Otis' belly is fully exposed. The back of his head is resting on my shoulder and all four legs are sticking straight out. I also know that it's best if I get to scratching him immediately or I am going to be getting an earful from him. First, he will start to moan then follow it up with some sort of strange sounding gurgle. If I still haven't started scratching, Odd Otis will follow the moaning-gurgle up with a low growl, which of course is his best shot at giving me a fake warning. Odd Otis knows it and I know it, but one must sometimes just play along.

Ever since the wife's retirement whenever it's snowing, raining, or looks nasty outside I look for a place to hide or a task to take on that makes me look like I'm busy. If I don't, Kathi will find something for me to do that is guaranteed to be anything but fun. That being said, after I finish my office business in the morning I like to sneak off to the living room for a bit of reading. I think it's a good way to get the day off to a fresh start and it makes me look like I'm doing something that's somewhat productive, or at the least—Intellectual. Though this keeps Kathi at bay it fails to work with Odd Otis. Reading turns out to be yet another doggie ritual that's slowly solidifying itself into stone.

Every morning it's a race to see who gets into my lap first. Will it be Odd Otis or will it be Winchester? Even though Odd Otis is blind and deaf, he almost always wins. I am beginning to think that Chester really doesn't have his heart in it, or it could be that he doesn't have all of his butt in it. When it comes to getting into a chair a Basset is somewhat handicapped with their long body and extremely short legs. I probably should figure out some type of handicap system like they do in golf, but I'm pretty sure that Odd Otis would not stand for it. He would most likely appeal his case to the *Race for the Lap* committee… whomever and where ever they might be.

Kathi and I have learned to never make the mistake of underestimating Odd Otis. His special needs have sharpened those senses that are still in good working order and have, therefore, increased his sensory input for smell and touch tenfold. Humans have approximately five million scent receptors while dogs have around 220 million. A fact I derived from my "intellectual" reading material. This means Odd Otis' escalated scenting ability is probably off the charts.

For Odd Otis touch rates as being the most important of all of his senses. He, like all dogs, has sensory hairs embedded in areas of his skin that are able to determine the shape and texture of the objects around him. This helps him learn where walls and furniture are so that he doesn't run into them. Another fact derived from my "intellectual" reading material.

My learning about Odd Otis' sharpened senses has also helped explain the birth of his skills as a doggie con artist. Diversion is his favorite M.O. (modus operandi) for any con that he might be planning. For example, he's learned how to get what he wants by luring the Bassets into a false sense of security. "How's that possible?" one might ask. He starts off with "Hey Bassets, I'm gonna clean your ears for'ya." Then he follows it up with "…and when I'm done with that, I'm gonna clean your eyes too." The Bassets lay back in a relaxed state of ecstasy while Odd Otis patiently licks their ears and eyes.

Their Basset eyeballs eventually begin to roll back into their heads and they slowly sink into a state of blissful oblivion. It's at this point that the con artist in Odd Otis takes over.... he jumps up and grabs whatever it is he's really been after all along; a half-chewed bone, a toy, and/or the best chair in the living room. The funny thing is that he never tires of this con and the Bassets have not yet figured it out. Maybe we should change his name to *Bamboozle*.

Poor Odd Otis does have his problems though. Gads, who doesn't? We all have to go to work and then pay Uncle Sam for the privilege. Right? Anyway, work and taxes are thankfully not challenges that Odd Otis needs to deal with. A hard and calloused sore nose, however, is. The poor guy has spent all of his years using it as a bumper guard to help guide him through a congested world, making it inevitable that sooner or later it's going to start showing signs of wear and tear. Though he has learned to navigate his way around the furniture and walls in our home, he still runs into anything that has been moved, dropped, or laid down. Worse yet, if he gets overly excited about something he tends to lose his bearings. When this happens the area surrounding him suddenly becomes an unfamiliar maze. We researched the internet and found a doggie device for blind dogs called a 'Halo'. It's a large hoop that attaches to the collar at the back of the dog's head and protrudes a few inches past his nose. The hoop lets the dog know when there's an object in front of him... before he runs into it. Though this is a great invention for most blind dogs, we were afraid the Bassets would think it was a toy and grab onto it, then drag poor Odd Otis around the house. So we decided instead to soothe his poor dry cracked nostrils with a little Vaseline. Fortunately, it only took a couple of days before his bumper-power was back in bumping business.

As we mentioned earlier in our story, the first thing the Bassets showed Odd Otis was the door....the dog door that is. We were totally amazed at how quickly Odd Otis figured out how he needed to go through the living room, through the kitchen, down the hallway, into Kathi's office and turn left, exit through the little door with the flap, go past the deck, through the gate, and into the gravel-covered area of the backyard to do his business. I can't even begin to tell you how long it took us to teach this same mapped route to the Bassets. Even after Winchester had the route down to a tee, we still had to help him understand that when he went out to do his business, he had to go ALL THE WAY OUT the dog door… not half-way out. Mysterious pee spots had been showing up on the throw rug lying inside and in front of the doggie-door exit. Winchester figured that as long as his head and front legs were outside, everything else must be a go (literally).

Odd Otis sometimes likes to nap under our bed with just his four legs protruding from underneath the bed skirt. That in itself looks odd, but what looks even odder is when a dream kicks in and all four of his protruding legs start running. We're guessing it's a breed thing and that he must either be counting or herding sheep. When he's not napping under the bed, he likes to curl up next to our feet and nap with one paw placed firmly on top of one of our feet. His foot fetish seems to be his preferred napping place whenever we are sitting, standing, and/or are otherwise immobile. This includes, but is not limited to, while we are watching TV, trying to prepare something in the kitchen, brushing our teeth, and/or trying to accomplish other bathroom business. Though we get that he's an Australian Shepherd mix and they are genetically known to be herders, we aren't quite sure that this qualifies as a breed thing. We are sure though that it's his way of keeping tabs on us.

Odd Otis doesn't know how to play one-on-one with us. Remember, he's never seen or heard an exchange of play between humans and dogs. Consequently, when he gets excited and wants to include us in the fun he rears up and down on his two hind legs. Kind of like a bucking horse. It's an odd thing to watch and exceptionally funny. Odd Otis' odd sense of play does not stop there, it continues on with his favorite thing to play with…a throw rug. We call it rug wrestling. Odd Otis rug wrestles at least, ten times a day. He uses his teeth to grab hold of the small throw rug that we've made available to him in the guest room (he has lots of wrestling room in there) then he wrestles with it. He wraps and unwraps himself in it, kicks it up in the air with his hind feet and then rolls around and bites it…then kicks it up in the air again. All while he's making some kind of odd guttural and snorting noises. This can go on for a good five minutes or longer. We are guessing that this is either an odd form of play or it's a form of dominance over the only thing in the house that he knows he can physically whip.

Our annual trip to our excellent and thorough vet has been made. The Bassets rode in the back seat and Odd Otis sat on my lap. Booster shots were given, ears peered into, teeth examined, and fur covered bodies poked and probed with a poke and a probe. The Bassets, as always, were oblivious to the needle that Dr. Colyer poked into their backside. Odd Otis, on the other hand, didn't fare so well. Though his failure to see and hear any distractions is a plus at times, it's a minus when it comes to pain sensitivity. He cried like a baby. The good news was that Odd Otis got a clean bill of health. The bad news was that two of the Bassets needed a cyst removed and an expensive dental cleaning that required antiseptic. "Thank you, Alan and Kathi, and oh yeah here's your vet bill." Oh well, like I always say "when it comes to money it's *hard come and easy go* ".

Large bags of dog food and assorted dog cookies in varying flavors are purchased monthly. Extra toys and a doggie bed for Odd Otis have been bought and a new deck has been built with an attached overhang. We can't have Odd Otis and the Bassets getting wet when they go outside to do their business.

Did I forget to mention the second new deck? Too many pine trees prevent us from growing grass and "yes" Kathi tends to get a bit disconcerted when muddy paw prints in the winter and sticky pitch in the spring gets tracked into the house. So once again for *survival reasons* (mostly mine), a second new deck and five yards of gravel were added to the back yard. Odd Otis and the Bassets love their two decks... it's round and round we go until they are all pooped and ready for their fifth nap of the day. Which, of course, gives us humans the extra time we need to get our chores done… without the help of four curious wet nosed dogs.

Oh yes! To help cover the doggie costs I might mention how, on more than one occasion, I have suggested to Kathi that she apply for the graveyard shift at the local donut shop. Unfortunately for me, however, Kathi's response to my suggestion has never once been a very nice one. Oh well, I said it once and I'll say it again, "when it comes to money it's *hard come easy go*."

# The Upside to Being Deaf....The vacuum cleaner doesn't disturb Odd Otis' nap!

*As told by Kathi Hiatt*

Neither Alan nor I have been able to figure out why it is Odd Otis is not completely bald. I swear I have swept and sucked up enough white dog hair in the vacuum cleaner to build two more Odd Otis'. Whenever I drag out and turn on the *vacuum cleaner monster* the Bassets can't get out the doggie door and into the backyard fast enough. For Odd Otis, however, it's an upside to his special needs because he could care less. When he's napping on the carpet I can vacuum all around him and he just continues to snore. In fact, I can even hook up a brush attachment and vacuum him. He loves it. He wakes up just long enough to roll over so I don't miss his underbelly.

In spite of Odd Otis' overzealous willingness to be vacuumed, it still doesn't stop those embarrassing moments when we are socializing—Not only does everyone know we have a white dog, they also know he stands approximately twenty-six inches high. The telltale sign is the dog hair that covers our pant legs just above the knees and all the way down to our ankles. We've learned to *suck it up* though. Whoever came up with the slogan "No outfit is complete until it's covered in dog hair," must have had a white dog too.

In the last year or so that Alan and I have had Odd Otis, he has never had an accident in the house. Anyone who has ever trained a puppy can appreciate those bragging rights. As we mentioned earlier, when Odd Otis first arrived the Bassets taught him how to use the doggie door in my office. Odd Otis' keen sense of smell lets him know when he's outside of the house, and what room he's in when he's inside the house. So, the end result is that his heightened senses let him know exactly where his doggie business *end* needs to end up.

Though Odd Otis is taller than the Bassets, he weighs about the same. The reason I am making this comparison is because what started out to be cute little tootsie rolls when the Bassets were puppies, now looks like a couple of cows have somehow snuck into our back yard. I don't know exactly how it happened but, for some unknown reason, Alan always has been and continues to be the official family pooper scooper. Whenever he complains that he must be picking up eight pounds of dog poop a day (two pounds for each dog) I remind him that four dogs couldn't possibly poop more than three dogs. Right?

Winchester seems to be Odd Otis' designated interpreter. Whenever Alan and I come home or a visitor rings the doorbell Winchester hunts Odd Otis down for a nose-to-nose chit-chat. Odd Otis responds by jumping up and running to the front door where he waits until we or the visitor walks through it. Odd Otis loves new comers and old comers alike. He stands back with his nose up in the air until the Bassets are done with their enthusiastic and sometimes unwanted greetings—they have uncontrollable lickers. He then cautiously noses and sniffs the new arrival before sitting and waiting patiently for them to respond with a couple of pets. If only the Bassets were that courteous. I have tried on numerous occasions to get the Bassets to not greet us or our guests so enthusiastically, but obedience training must be consistent and Alan stinks at both obedience and consistency.

This is not to say that our dogs are allowed to completely run amuck. The Bassets were all ears (small pun) when I taught them to sit, go get in their beds, and the word "no"! Unfortunately, however, these are all verbal commands. So these directives fall on deaf ears when it comes to Odd Otis. Not to say, however, Odd Otis can't be trained. With perseverance and bribes (doggie cookies) we have taught him to sit with two taps on the nose, to shake with two taps on his right shoulder, and the word "no" with two taps on his back. He has also learned to run to the front door whenever we hold his leash up to his nose, which is where he sits and waits patiently for one of us to come and take him for a walk. Odd Otis actually responds to more commands than the Bassets do and, truth be told, he also learned quicker. No, not because he's smarter because as we all know there is only one *smarter* dog in the world and everyone else owns him— Because, unlike the Bassets, he doesn't see the visual distractions or hear the noise distractions that surround him. It's another upside to Odd Otis' special needs…he learns quickly.

Who learns *not so quickly* is us! For instance, we found out the hard way you cannot push or pull Odd Otis when you want him to come with you. He puts on his brakes and his fifty pound Australian Shepherd body instantly becomes two hundred pounds of dead weight. Unlike those of us who can see and hear what's in front of us, for Odd Otis it is a scary and unknown dark abyss. After a lot of trials and a lot of errors we eventually discovered that by placing the tips of our finger under his nose, it lets him know we are in the lead and he is willing to follow us anywhere. Evidently, he figures he will have enough advance warning if we fall into the dark abyss first. Unfortunately, it took a whole lot of pushing, pulling, and actually picking Odd Otis up and carrying him before we finally figured it out.

Doggie dental care is always a concern for a family with Basset Hounds. Slobber, bits of food, bug legs, and pieces of whatever stinky stuff they find on the ground has a tendency to linger in their jowls. This, unfortunately, can then lead to bacteria entering the gum line which can then lead to gum disease and/or tooth decay. In order to avoid future gum and teeth problems, as well as a costly vet bill, we follow our vet's advice and purchases bones from a local butcher shop.

The Bassets are always happy to gnaw on their freshly purchased bones on the deck in the backyard. Odd Otis, however, was a different story. Fearing the Bassets would try and sneak his bone away from him, Odd Otis would try to hide it from them by burying it. Burying instead of chewing was not doing his teeth any good. Odd Otis, of course, had no way of knowing the Bassets were watching him while he dug his *secret hiding place* hole, nor did he realize that they were digging it back up as soon as he was done.

To help reassure Odd Otis no one was going to steal his bone, Alan decided to try isolating him away from the Bassets. He hooked Odd Otis up to a leader in the garage and then placed him and his bone on a large doggie pillow. It didn't work. Instead of chewing on the bone, Odd Otis insisted on trying to bury the bone in the pillow. Though he was isolated from the Bassets, we think Odd Otis was most likely still picking up the scents of our neighbor's dogs, and he was just sure they were going to sneak into the fenced yard, eat Alan and then steal his bone from him. Odd Otis had no way of knowing what fences even were, let alone how they were able to keep any possible intruders out.

In our continual efforts to get Odd Otis to chew and not bury his bone, we decided to try putting him on an old throw rug in the guest room. He would at least know he was safe from the Basset thieves, and wouldn't be subjected to neighbor dog smells. The upside to this solution was how it worked, he began chewing on his bone. The downside to this solution was how he wanted Alan to stand guard over him while he chewed. Whenever Alan attempted to walk away, Odd Otis would resort back to trying to find a good burial spot. Odd Otis' digging a hole in our new carpet was a sure-fire way to get both him and Alan banned to the doghouse in the backyard….. forever. Odd Otis for being a *digger* and Alan for being the one who brought the *digger* home!

Alan, of course, had no desire to stand guard over Odd Otis while he leisurely gnawed on his bone. So, he took off his shoes and socks and placed them next to a blind Odd Otis, hoping that it would trick Odd Otis' *smeller* into thinking he (Alan) was standing guard. It worked! Alan was able to go about his business and Odd Otis' teeth got the chewing they needed. The problem was solved!

We gave up trying to get Odd Otis to sleep with the Bassets, once we realized he was spending cold nights on the deck instead of on the pillow we had laid down for him in my office. Over the years the Bassets have made it a practice to trade beds all night long. Whenever one of the Bassets exits the doggie door to go potty and then returns, he/she usually finds that one of the other Bassets is now occupying his/her bed. No problem though, the now bed-less Basset simply lays claim to the bed that was vacated. Unfortunately for Odd Otis, however, when he exited to go potty and then returned to reclaim his now occupied bed, he was greeted with a warning growl. He couldn't see there was another empty bed available so he'd go back outside and curl up on a deck pillow. As we mentioned earlier, it gets icy cold up here in the winter. We had no choice, we had to make some immediate changes.

Though the Bassets continue to bed down at night behind the closed door to my office, Odd Otis now has full run of the house. He has since decided on approximately five different sleeping spots that he likes to alternate back and forth in *all night long*. How do we know this? Because we hear his toenails clicking on the laminate flooring *all night long.*

In order to make the house and yard safe for Odd Otis, we have had to make a few adjustments. For instance, Odd Otis seems to be claustrophobic so we had to bungee cord the bathroom door open to keep him from accidentally locking himself in. While investigating the guest bathroom he accidentally broke the glass Kleenex holder sitting on the back of the toilet so we replaced it with a metal one. To protect his nose from any possible burn damage, we purchased two fireplace screens and placed them in front of the pellet and propane stoves. In order to protect his sensitive eyes from flying bugs, low-lying bushes, and the sun we went on-line and found him a pair of red doggie-goggles (Doggles) to wear. He likes them because he thinks they make him look just like Snoopy.

Our home has four steps leading down to an enclosed sun room and the same number of steps leading up to the deck in the backyard. Because steps are a danger to blind dogs, we opted to show him where they were instead of closing them off. I'm happy to report that Odd Otis has not accidentally fallen down or up them...not even once.

In spite of all of our efforts to make Odd Otis' surrounding safe, we still had a scary moment when he got caught under the deck in the back yard. He let us and the entire neighborhood know he wanted out NOW! We have since covered the hole he crawled through and the whole incident served as a reminder to secure other possible problem areas in both the yard and the house.

Thanks to these few minor adjustments Odd Otis is now able to skillfully zigzag throughout the house and yard with as much ease as the Bassets. His nose barely brushes against the walls and furniture as he glides by, over, and around the obstacles that surround him. When we meet Odd Otis head-on in the hallway we simply bow our legs and he glides right through them. The only thing we still haven't been able to *Odd Otis proof* are the Bassets. Whenever he accidentally runs into one of them (which happens frequently) he gets a low "Hey! Watch where you're going?" growl which he, of course, can't hear.

Though Odd Otis may need a little extra attention and help with his special needs, he is just as loving and capable as any other dog. For the most part, Odd Otis can pretty much do all the things other dogs can do. In spite of the severity of his special needs, he has proven he can be trained as successfully and easily as any dog. Odd Otis is a sweet and loving friend to everyone and every animal he meets and greets. He is full of *doggie spirit* and makes us laugh on a daily basis. He's an inspiration and a walking reminder for all of us to appreciate and hold dearly our gifts of sight and sound. Odd Otis, like the rest of our dog children, *never* passes judgment, *never* holds a grudge, *never* puts himself first and most important of all… he will *never* be a teenager.

*Odd Otis thinks he is being guarded from predators (Basset Hounds) while he chews on his bone! He doesn't know there's no one wearing those shoes.*

# Epilogue

*Warm Hearts & Cold Noses Make a Home*

The story of Odd Otis continues to unfold on a daily basis. He still favors morning office time in Alan's lap, while the Bassets prefer morning naps in the living room. After all, having to get up to eat breakfast can be quite tiring and the living room offers the closest place to bed down.

The Bassets have since learned to respect Odd Otis and each other's eating areas, which means we no longer have to stand guard over Odd Otis' bowl. This is a good thing as it also means we are no longer subjected to the "thank you" licks Odd Otis likes to share after devouring dog food topped with three squirts of fish oil.

Oh, and it's now official. Odd Otis is the designated family groomer and hygienist. Both Lucy and Chester have decided to share the alpha dog role, except when Kathi steps in… then they abdicate to her. Abby is content with just sitting in her chair (which used to be Alan's chair) and watching the events of the day unfold. She's the quiet-silent type.

Tina calls and comes by now and then. Sometimes she even brings Odd Otis' sister, Twiggy. Twiggy is blind, but not deaf. She looks a lot like Odd Otis except she's smaller and much more hyper than him. Several months ago Tina brought Twiggy over with a casted broken leg. The pit bull who had Tina worried because of his potential mean streak attacked Twiggy and broke her leg in half. Poor Twiggy must have been terrified. We shudder when we think about what could have happened to Odd Otis…Tina is sure he would have jumped in to protect Twiggy. We are just happy it was a decision Odd Otis never had to make. Twiggy's leg has since healed and she's doing fine, thank goodness.

Back when Odd Otis first came to live with us, we had asked ourselves what our part in all of this was going to be. We now have an answer to that question. If it wasn't for Odd Otis we would never have been inspired to write this book or share with the rest of the world the wonderful adventure this dog has taken us on. Odd Otis has redefined for us what it means to retire and taught us to pursue our newly found passion for advocating for the adoption of special needs dogs. Through him, we have reinvented ourselves and are doing what we can to promote others to adopt dogs like Odd Otis.

More recently we have taken Odd Otis to schools where we encourage children to exercise kindness and patience when dealing with both special need animals and people; and to adult organizations where we promote the adoption of special need animals. We remember reading (somewhere in our retirement handouts) how *too much leisure time is often an expressway to boredom and unhappiness......*

"Thank You" Odd Otis for taking us on this special needs journey, because we can honestly say "**we are neither of those two things!**"

# Odd Otis Goes to School…

and teaches patience and tolerance for special needs animals and people.

# Odd Otis
# Question & Answer's

*Odd Otis' most frequently asked questions....*

### How is Odd Otis different from other dogs?

Though dogs like Odd Otis may need a little extra attention and help to live with their special needs, they are just as loving and capable as any other dog. Much like a human, their deficiencies in the senses they have lost increases the efficiency in the senses they have not lost. For the most part, Odd Otis can pretty much do anything a normal dog can do. Even though he is a special needs dog, he can be trained as successfully and easily as any normal dog. All it takes is a loving and caring family.

### Will Odd Otis bite if you startle him?

Does he "startle" when you unexpectedly touch him? Yes. Does he bite? Absolutely not. Because his world has been dark and silent since birth Odd Otis has adapted to his sight and hearing loss. Having said that, however, we have to assume that because **we** don't like being startled it is most likely uncomfortable for him as well. Therefore, we try to remember to toe-tap the floor twice (he can feel the vibration) before touching him unexpectedly. That way he knows a touch is coming.

### Is Odd Otis house broken?

Yes. Though the Bassets taught Odd Otis to use the doggie door, we now know that even without their help, we still could have easily trained him to do his business outside. Even though Odd Otis can't see or hear, he knows what "no" means (two taps on his back). His elevated sense of touch helps him determine where he is at by whatever it is he feels under his paws (carpet, tile, gravel driveway, grass, etc.). His keen sense of smell also lets him know when he's outside of the house and what room he is in when he is inside the house. Like any normal dog, Odd Otis responds well to any reward for good behavior which includes treats and/or hugs of approval.

### If Odd Otis happens to wander off, how will anyone know he is blind and deaf?

We ordered a special collar on-line for Odd Otis. It is bright yellow and has the words *deaf and blind* imprinted on it. Odd Otis is also micro-chipped and wears a tag with our name and phone number. Other precautions we have taken, in order to make sure he doesn't wander off, has been fencing the back yard and never letting Odd Otis off of a leash when we have him out and about.

### How does Odd Otis know when it's night and time to go to bed?

Odd Otis' a.m. and p.m. is ruled by routine. Every night he joins Kathi in the bathroom while she takes a shower. He then waits for her to fill his water bowl and place it next to the bathtub; then lay his blanket next to Alan's side of the bed. Once these tasks are accomplished he settles in on his blanket and calls it a night. His alarm clock in the morning is the smell of coffee brewing.

*Odd Otis can't hear, so why not change his name to Magoo?*

When Odd Otis lived with Tina she would whisper his name in his ear to soothe him whenever he was upset. We produce vibrations when we talk, so even though Odd Otis can't hear his name he does recognize the vibrations of our voice when we whisper in his ear. Consequently, he also feels the difference in how we pronounce our words. To change his name to "Magoo" would have been too confusing for him and, besides that, we think "Odd Otis" fits him better.

*Does Tina come over to visit with Odd Otis?*

Yes. Tina stops by often and sometimes she brings Twiggy over to visit too. Tina has become a close friend and she has recently rekindled her skills as an artist. She is working with us to publish an Odd Otis picture book for small children.

*Why was Odd Otis born blind and deaf?*

After doing a thorough online search we found a couple of sites that helped us come to understand the *whys and how's* of Odd Otis' special needs. Odd Otis is what breeders commonly refer to as a double merle or a lethal white. Both names were derived from the birth defects caused by irresponsible breeding.

*What is a double merle?*

Merle is a dominant gene that decides the pattern in a dog's coat. The merle gene creates mottled patches of color and can also affect eyes, ears and skin pigment. Sight and hearing issues are more typical and more severe when two merles are bred together. Consequently, it is recommended a merle be bred to a dog with a solid coat color only. The term double merle simply describes a pup that was born with two copies of the merle gene and is the result of breeding two merle dogs. It is important to know that not all double merle dogs are blind and not all are deaf. Very few are born blind and deaf like Odd Otis.

### What is a Lethal White?

Lethal white is a term that was originally described as a lethal gene found in certain types of horses. These horses are born white with blue eyes and die within a few hours to a few days after their birth. More recently, the *Lethal White* term is also sometimes used to describe certain breeds of dogs, including Australian Shepherds. Lethal white pups have been historically destroyed at birth because they are born blind, deaf or both. Unlike horses, however, blind and/or deaf pups born with the double merle gene are otherwise healthy and able to develop normally. They typically do not die shortly after birth. Consequently, in some circles, referring to double merle dogs as lethal whites is considered insulting. This, however, is only because some folks feel the negative implications brought on by the term *Lethal White* tends to discourage prospective dog adoptions. The other side of this issue claims that the term *lethal white* promotes awareness and prompts prospective adoptions of special needs dogs.

### Are there other breeds of dogs, besides Australian Shepherds, that carry the double merle gene?

Yes. Other breeds of dogs that may be subject to the double merle gene are Cocker Spaniels, Sheepdogs, Pomeranians, Collies, Chihuahuas, Dachshunds, and Pit Bull Terriers. Because breeding merle to merle dogs produces a patterned coat that is popular with dog owners, breeders continue to introduce the merle gene into different breeds. Unfortunately, merle to merle breeding produces litters with as many as 25% of the puppies being born with severe disabilities.

*Is the double merle gene the cause of other health issues?*

No. It has not been proven that the double merle gene effects anything other than eyes, ears, and skin. Any other health problems Odd Otis may encounter (allergies, tumors, internal organ problems, shorter life span, etc.) are the same health risks any normal dog faces. The only physical characteristics retained in all breeds of dogs is that they all have ears, a nose, and a leg in each corner.

*Would you consider adopting another special needs dog like Odd Otis?*

Absolutely! In fact, we have decided that from this point on, all of our rescued dogs will be special needs. Through Odd Otis, we have reinvented ourselves in a wonderfully positive way. We have learned that adopting a special needs dog has been as rewarding for us as it was fortunate for Odd Otis.

*Where do I go to adopt or foster a special needs dog?*

There are too many animal rescue groups to list them all, but one option is to use the internet to do a search by breed for special needs or search *Special Needs Dog Adoptions.* Several sites from all over the country will pop up. You can also contact your local animal shelter and let them know you are interested in adopting or fostering a special needs dog. They will be happy to hear from you.

*What can I do to help, if I'm unable to adopt or foster a special needs dog?*

Rescue groups and shelters are always in need of monetary contributions, as well as dog food, bowls, blankets, etc. A donation of your time at one of your local animal shelters is yet another way to help.

# ODD OTIS
# TOUCH COMMANDS

Because Odd Otis cannot see or hear, we use touch commands to show him what it is that we want him to do. For instance, to teach Odd Otis to *sit* we simply tapped his nose twice, then lured him into a sitting position, and immediately followed it up with a doggie treat and a *"good boy"* hug. We repeated this technique three more times. We repeated the entire exercise, at least, three times each day. In a short period of time, Odd Otis was sitting when we tapped his nose.

We utilized this same technique for all of the other commands that we have taught Odd Otis to do, including *down, no, shake, etc.* Please keep in mind, however, that though they are important for training purposes, we cut treats into small pieces so that Odd Otis stays at a healthy weight.

Odd Otis learned quickly but, like humans, every dog is different and some learn a little faster or slower than others. Patience is extremely important. Five to ten minutes a day, three times a day is plenty of training time. If your dog is easily overwhelmed, we suggest you reduce the number of times per day to once. We would also recommend teaching only one command at a time, and that everyone in the family always uses the same touch sequence to mean the same thing. Trying to teach more than one command at a time, or mixing up touch sequences can be confusing for the dog and frustrating for us humans.

No dog door? We were fortunate enough to have our Bassets teach Odd Otis how to use the dog door, but what if you don't have a Basset and a dog door? You can teach any dog to let you know when he needs to go outside. One popular way is to hang a bell for him to touch or ring with his nose or paw. For blind and deaf dogs you may want to utilize the touch command techniques by first leading your dog to the door, luring him into ringing the bell, taking him outside to do his business, then rewarding him with a treat **after** he has done his business. If he goes outside and doesn't do his business, it's best not to give him a treat. Bring him back in and wait before taking him out again. Remember, patience is important. All dogs are anxious to please, they just need to learn to connect-the-dots (understand) what it is you want them to do. *WARNING*.. If you reward your dog with a treat right *after* he rings the bell and *before* he does his business, he may think he is being rewarded for simply going outside. Needless to say, you could quickly become a revolving door and subjected to listening to a ringing bell **all day long**.

# THE AUTHORS INSPIRATION

Prior to having dogs the Hiatt's owned two *outside* cats (Tasha and Morgan) and a Rex rabbit they named Miss Mulligan. The "Miss" was added after the veterinarian informed them *he* was a *she*.

Tasha was a petite and sweet long haired calico. She was living with Alan when he first started dating Kathi. Alan still claims Tasha is the only female in his life who has never given him any sass. This, of course, is a jovial affront directed at Kathi and their three daughters.

Morgan was a twenty pound (no, that was not a typo) orange Tom Cat who had originally belonged to one of their daughters. Morgan came to live with the Hiatts after the daughter enlisted in the Army. Happily, both cats and the rabbit made it well into and through their senior years before passing peacefully away.

On a number of occasions Alan and Kathi had talked about getting a dog, but it had always been just that.... talk. Kathi is a neat freak and so is Alan. Consequently, the thought of dog hair, chewed up table legs, and cleaning puppy poop off of the carpet did not appeal to either one of them. Besides that, their girls were grown and gone, and for the first time in years there was a place for everything and everything was in its place. The Hiatts just didn't meet any of the criteria required to become *dog people*. In fact, they were such unlikely candidates for the *dog people* title, even their closest of friends were in shock when they brought Theodore home.

Theodore, according to both Hiatts, was the cutest puppy in the whole world. He was a full blooded Basset Hound with long ears he constantly tripped over and a face that would have melted *Helen of Troy*. Theodore was their pride and joy, and they loved him...**a lot!**

Though it was supposed to be for only one night, Theodore's permanent sleeping spot quickly became the middle of the Hiatt's bed. A new carpet shampooer had been purchased and was sitting next to the vacuum cleaner in the hall closet. There were holes in their perfectly manicured lawn; chewed-up flip-flops were under the bed and a sticky mixture of dog hair and slobber coated the arms of their sofa. The Hiatts had officially become *dog people*.

Theodore has since crossed over the Rainbow Bridge, and the Hiatts have since adopted and rescued several amazing dogs. But it was Theodore (they say) who showed them how to laugh every day and taught them a dog's definition of unconditional love and trust. Theodore continues to be a part of their on-going inspiration for all that they do to help raise awareness for rescuing dogs, including adopting Odd Otis and writing this book.

Theodore remains in a special place in both of their hearts. Neither of them hesitates when they say, "we still do and always will love him**...a lot**!"

# Author Resources
## For
## Bling/Deaf Dogs

**BOOKS**
*Through a Dark Silence, Loving and Living with Your Blind and Deaf Dog* By Debbie Bauer was published in 2014 and is available on Amazon.com Books and Barnes & Nobles

*Blind Devotion, Enhancing the Lives of Blind and Visually Impaired Dogs* By Cathy Symons was published in 2012 and is available on Amazon.com Books in Paperback

**WEBSITES**
A downloadable brochure is available on *An Introduction to White Aussies* that carry the Merle gene at www.whiteaussies.com

How to Care for Blind and Deaf Senior Dogs
www.petplace.com/article/dogs/pet-care/how-to-care-for-blind-and-deaf-senior-d...

Lethal Whites UK offers information on special need dogs born with the Merle gene at www.lethalwhitesuk.webs.com

**PRODUCTS FOR SPECIAL NEEDS DOGS**
www.handicappedPets.com is a wonderful resource for a wide array of specially designed pet products for pets with special needs

**BLIND AND DEAF DOG GROUPS ON FACEBOOK**
Like these sites: *Blind and Deaf Dogs Networking*
*Blind/Deaf & Other Special Needs Shelter Dogs*
Click groups:   *Blind and Deaf Dog Owners*
*Blind Dogs – Owners and Supporters*

Friend *Odd Otis* on FaceBook

# THANK YOU!

**We Hope You Enjoyed Odd Otis!**

**Please Help Future Readers by Leaving a Review on Amazon.com Books**

# ODD OTIS

## Amazon Book 5-STAR Reviews

*"...a wonderful, true, heartwarming story and the dog doesn't die. For all who have been blessed enough to be the companion of a special needs dog, this story will fill you with joy & appreciation for the magic in skin to fur contact."*

*"I thought this was one of the most entertaining books I've ever read, & I thoroughly enjoyed it! Having a "teleporting alien" of my own, I could definitely relate to the problems they had keeping him in the yard. Odd Otis is adorable and he and his owners have definitely made a wonderful family for him. Anyone who loves dogs will fall in love with Odd Otis."*

*"We have a blind but hearing dog and can relate to this story. Special needs dog's rock! Anyone considering adopting a special needs dog needs to read this."*

*"I recently adopted a blind and deaf dog so I could totally relate to some of the situations. I really enjoyed reading this book. Not much material is out there about blind and/or deaf dogs and I felt so helpless when I adopted my girl. Now I know there are others that have gone through similar trials and tribulations as me. I would trade any of the trials for the world. Thank you for sharing."*

*"This was a marvelous story. I plan on getting a copy for my Great- Grandson."*

*"I was attracted to this book because the authors live nearby, and also because I readily read books about dogs. Odd Otis, Alan and Kathi diligent search to locate his owner after Alan found Odd Otis stranded on the Skyway - Odd Otis was incredibly lucky, folks drive up the Skyway as if they were running from the devil! The story was charming and heart-warming, and hats off to the Hiatt's for the Epilogue in which they encourage the adoption of handicapped dogs, and in which they describe the negative impact of allowing deleterious genes to remain in the canine breeding population".*

*"I just finished reading Odd Otis, a cleverly written, humorous review of life with this puppy with special needs. Most impressive is the deep empathy and concern felt by the adopted owners."*

*"This is a true story that was meant to happen and be told. This shows us what can go wrong with breeding but can go right with the outcome. Odd Otis is the Helen Keller of the dog world. He shows us that regardless of the infirmities dealt to us in life we can communicate love and be loved in return."*

*"A delightful read, funny and sad. Odd Otis is very lucky to have such loving and caring people like Alan and Kathi in his life and I'm sure they feel like the lucky ones. A must read."*

*"This is a heartwarming story about a special needs dog and the family of 2 adults and 3 dogs that lovingly welcome him into their home and life. A must read for all animal lovers!!"*

*"A wonderful heartwarming reminder that people aren't the only ones with special needs. Odd Otis will make you smile and get a little teary eyed. This is a quick read so take a little time to get to know Odd Otis and his family. You'll be glad you did."*

*"I just finished reading Odd Otis and what an enjoyable read it was. It made me laugh out loud and having to wipe away a tear or two from time to time. This is a must have book for all animal lovers. I highly recommend it. I also like it that the authors are donating proceeds of their book to the ASPCA to promote awareness that special needs dogs are just as capable and loving as any other dog."*

*"Loved it! Borrowed this from my sister and so glad I did! I'm a lover of dogs as it is and Odd Otis has stolen my heart. The way this is written by the two different dog parents was great. I highly recommend!"*

*"I downloaded & read this book last night & I think it's just wonderful! I really enjoyed it. It made me laugh out loud several times & get a little happy-weepy as well! Sigh...I love books like that. I also love that the authors are donating a large portion of their proceeds to a good cause and how they are promoting the adoption of special needs animals."*

*"I've met Odd Otis; he is just a great dog. This is the first time I've heard his story, though - and enjoyed it very much. Read this book - it's heartwarming and funny. And, the "doggie parents" are just as nice as you think they will be. I really liked this book!"*

# On Amazon.com Books

\* \* \*

**Odd Otis**, A Special Needs Dog Who Doesn't Know He's Special Needs

*By*
*Award Winning Author*
*Kathleen T. Hiatt*

*A fun picture book for children ages 2-10*

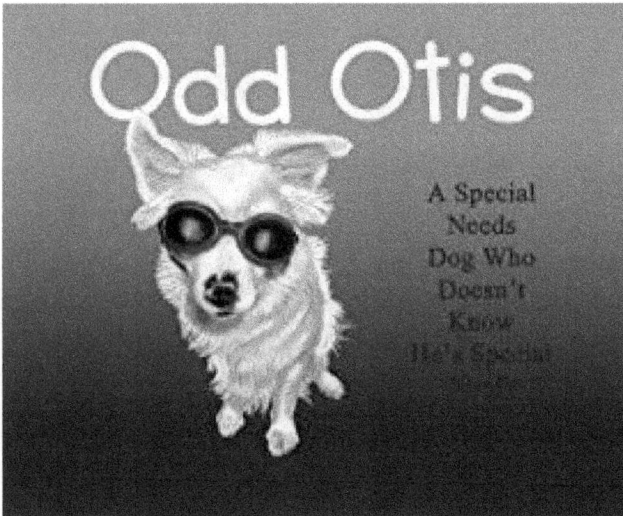

# A Long Story Short

American Literary Fiction

*By*
*Award Winning Author*
*Kathleen T. Hiatt*

*An award winning and published collection of short and original tales with unexpected endings*

# THE END

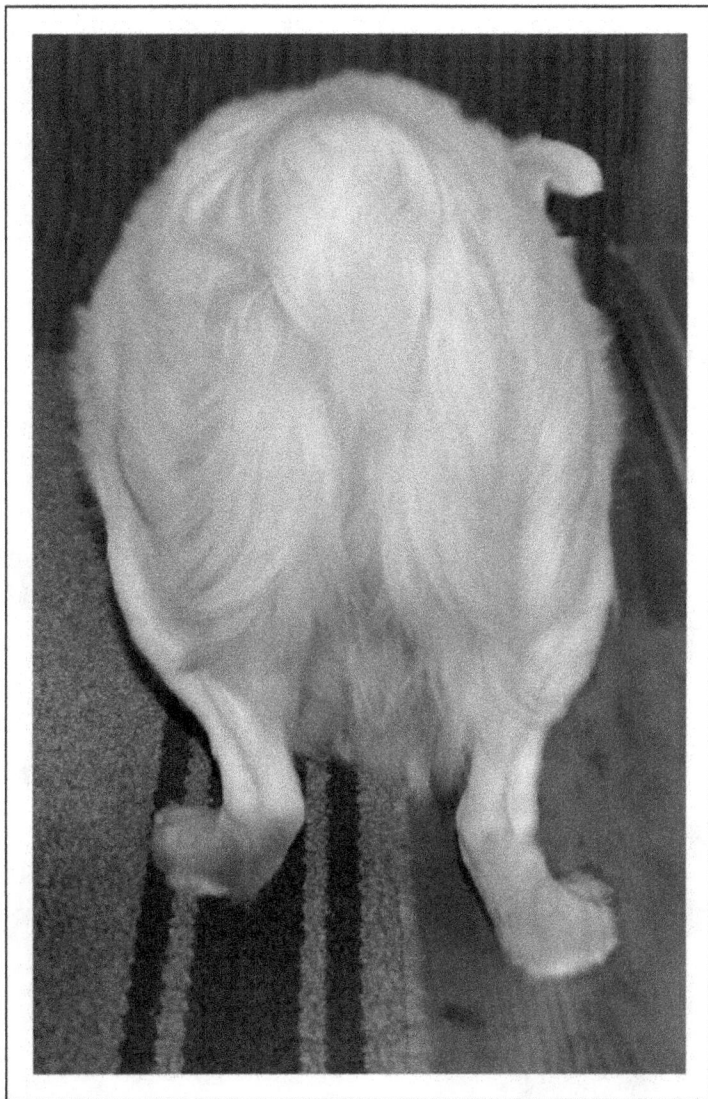

www.ingramcontent.com/pod-product-compliance
Lightning Source LLC
Chambersburg PA
CBHW050540280326
41933CB00011B/1660